ANTHOLOGY

OF

NEW NETHERLAND

ANTHOLOGY

OF

NEW NETHERLAND

OR

TRANSLATIONS FROM THE EARLY DUTCH POETS OF NEW YORK

WITH

𝔐emoirs of their 𝔏ives

BY

HENRY C. MURPHY

IRA J. FRIEDMAN, Inc.
Port Washington, L.I., N.Y.

ANTHOLOGY OF NEW NETHERLAND

Originally published in 1865 by The Bradford Club
Reissued in 1969 by Ira J. Friedman, Inc.
Library of Congress Catalog Card No: 74-101019
SBN 87198-071-1

Manufactured by Taylor Publishing Company   Dallas, Texas

EMPIRE STATE HISTORICAL PUBLICATIONS SERIES No. 71

TO

HON. GULIAN C. VERPLANCK

THIS VOLUME IS INSCRIBED

AS A

TESTIMONY OF HIS ZEAL IN BEHALF OF THE

LITERATURE OF FATHERLAND,

AND AS A

MARK OF PERSONAL ESTEEM

BY HIS FRIEND,

THE AUTHOR.

THE BRADFORD CLUB.

Under this designation, a few gentlemen interested in the study of American History and Literature, propose occasionally to print limited editions of such manuscripts and scarce pamphlets as may be deemed of value towards illustrating these subjects. They will seek to obtain, for this purpose, unpublished journals or correspondence containing matter worthy of record, and which may not properly be included in the Historical Collections or Documentary Histories of the several states. Such unpretending cotemporary chronicles often throw precious light upon the motives of action, and the imperfectly narrated events of by-gone days; perhaps briefly touched upon in dry official documents.

The Club may also issue fac-similes of curious manuscripts, or documents worthy of notice, which, like the printed issues, will bear its imprint.

> " These are the
> Registers, the chronicles of the age
> They were written in, and speak the truth of History
> Better than a hundred of your printed
> Communications." — *Shakerly Marmyon's Antiquary.*

William Bradford, the first New York Printer, whose name they have adopted, came to this country in 1682, and established his press in the neighborhood of Philadelphia. In 1693 he removed to this city, and set up the first press " at the sign of the Bible." His first work, printed in this colony, was entitled " the Laws and Acts of the General Assembly." During a period of thirty years he was the only Printer in the Province, and in his imprints he styled himself " Printer to the King." In 1725 he printed our first newspaper, *The New York Gazette.* He continued the business of his profession until within a few years of his death, which occurred in 1752, at the age of 92 years. He was described in an obituary notice of the day as " a man of great sobriety and industry, a real friend to the poor and needy, and kind and affable to all."

APRIL, 1859.

INTRODUCTION.

The purpose of this volume is to present to its readers the earliest poems written within the bounds of the state of New York, so far as is known. These were produced while the country was under the jurisdiction of the government of the United Provinces of the Netherlands. They are all the compositions of Hollanders born, and have hitherto existed only in the Dutch language; most of them now see the light, even in that language, for the first time; and none of them have ever before been rendered into English. Though not devoid of poetical merit, they are deemed at least of sufficient historical interest and importance to be entitled to preservation in this form; commemorating, as they do, the first essays in the art upon our own soil, and especially illustrating the nature of the country, and the character, habits and manners, both generally and particularly, of our first settlers, as well as their perils and dangers. Taken as a whole, they may be said, from the facts and events they narrate, to constitute our first epic, simple, unpretending, and perhaps wanting in high excellence, yet truthful and spirited in description. If the early ballads of a nation are, as has been well observed, inval-

uable for its history, how should these more authentic
pieces commend themselves to our precious care?

A few years ago, while sojourning in Holland, we
printed, for the gratification of a few friends, the
memoir and poems of Jacob Steendam, one of the
writers here referred to. The prefatory note to that
publication will best serve as an introduction to
further explanations.

"A miscellaneous volume of old placards and pro-
clamations of the States General and other broadsides,
put together, apparently, because they were all of the
same size, was sold a few months since at the Hague
at the public sale of a library. Bound up with this
rubbish of two centuries ago was a sheet of verses
on New Amsterdam, signed, "Jacob Steendam, *noch
vaster*." It was a lamentation over the neglect which
that new settlement had received at the hands of the
powerful city of Amsterdam, whose name it bore and
from which it was planted. A perusal of it excited
our suspicions that it was actually written by a colonist
and had been sent hence to the parental city for publication; and upon investigation those facts were fully
established. It is, as far as is yet known, the first
attempt at poetry in what are now the states of New
York, New Jersey and Delaware, and portions of the
states of Connecticut and Pennsylvania, containing a
population of European descent, at the present time,
of nearly twice that of the kingdom of the Netherlands; and has hitherto escaped all observation. The

author, however, was not altogether unknown to
fame in his native country; and his name is duly
registered in the anthology of Fatherland among the
four thousand poets whose works are found in print.
He had published a respectable volume of odes and
epithalamiums, and a small poem, called the "Praise
of New Netherland," together with sundry fugitive
pieces, among which was one with the quaint title of
"Spurring-verses to the Friends of the Colony and
Brotherhood to be established on the South River of
New Netherland." But the only biographical notice of
him to be found, is a short paragraph or two of fifteen
lines in Van der Aa's supplement to Witsen Geysbeek's
Dictionary of Dutch poets, in all respects imperfect
and unsatisfactory. The poems relating to New Netherlands are all exceedingly rare; and it seemed therefore not improper to ascertain if possible some further
particulars of the life of the poet, and, by a repro-
duction of the poems themselves, to save them from
the danger of being entirely lost. This has now been
done; and a translation added, which pretends to no
other merit than to convey the meaning of the poet,
in the same metrical forms as he himself adopted, for
the satisfaction of such friends into whose hands this
little publication may come, as may be unacquainted
with the Dutch language.

"In endeavoring to trace the career of Steendam, it
became necessary to resort to original sources for
materials. The labor has not been wholly without

fruit; but it has not resulted in as much as could have been desired. To the kindness of Dr. O'Callaghan of Albany, whose intimate acquaintance and long official connection with the colonial records there, entitle him to be considered the Archivist of the state of New York, we are indebted for the facts disclosed in regard to the poet's residence in the colony. J. T. Bodel Nijenhuis Esq. of Leyden brought to our notice the Spurring-verses; and his thorough knowledge of the poetry and literature of his country has also availed us in some valuable suggestions in preparing the memoir. Mr. Frederick Muller of Amsterdam, politely placed at our disposal the only portrait of Steendam, which we have seen, and has enabled us to present the semblance of the poet. There is Steendam! in his simple garb, a study of the costume of our early colonists; and in his frank and fearless countenance the type of the early settlers of New York. We were unwilling to leave any sources within our reach unexplored where any information might possibly exist for our purpose, and hence examinations have been made in the Royal Library and the National Archives at the Hague; and particularly in the latter among the records of the East India Company, for the purpose of discovering the end of the poet's wandering life. And, although little was elicited in those quarters, our thanks are nevertheless here due, for the unvarying courtesy and assistance which we received in the prosecution of our inquiries, to the gentlemen who administer the affairs of those two noble institutions, both as principals and in subordinate capacities.

" The reprints of the original poems descriptive of New Netherland are made from copies derived from different sources. The Complaint of New Amsterdam is from the copy in our possession, discovered in the manner above mentioned. The Praise of New Netherland is from a manuscript which we made ourselves several years ago, — not dreaming then of its use in this way or of the interest which now attaches to it, — from a printed copy belonging to James Lenox Esq. of New York, the only copy of the original edition we have been able to discover. The Spurring-Verses are from a copy in the Royal Library at the Hague, of the work of Pieter Cornelisz. Plockhoy, mentioned in the sketch of Steendam.

" In concluding this introduction we venture to express the hope that the poems of the Rev. Henricus Selyns, the second of the New Netherland poets, may be collected and published. He succeeded Steendam by a few years, having gone to the colony in 1660, where he was installed the first settled minister of Brooklyn in September of that year. Domine Selyns was one of the most accomplished scholars of his time; and was a poet and philosopher as well as a divine. There are some memorials of him here in Holland and some fugitive pieces of his poetry. There are also some lines of his prefixed to Mather's *Magnalia*. But it is not generally known that there is, or was a few years ago in New York, a manuscript volume of his poems, containing some verses of local interest, and among them two nuptial odes upon the marriage of Aegidius Luyck, rector of the Latin school in New Amsterdam in 1663, with Judith van Isendoorn; and also an epitaph upon Anna Loockermans, the widow of Olof Stevensz. van Cortlandt. It would be an interesting addition to the early poetry of our country, could this volume be made public; and the life of the author, who enjoyed a correspondence with Senguerdius, the learned professor of Natural Philosophy, and Willem-a-Brakel, the orthodox author of the *Redelijk Godsdienst*, — the most esteemed work perhaps in the whole range of Dutch theology, — would be a not less valuable contribution to the literature and scientific history of the United States. The Hague, 27 February, 1861."

At the time this was written, we hardly expected that the hope expressed in the concluding paragraph, of the recovery of the poems of Selyns, would be soon, if ever, realized. The last trace of the manuscript was in the hands of the author of Knickerbocker's New York, at the time he was engaged in writing his travestie of the history of New Netherland. In December, 1854, in a letter to James Lenox, Esq., Mr. Irving says: "There must be somewhere extant a small volume of Dutch poems in manuscript, very neatly copied out, relating to persons and events in New Amsterdam, in the early times of the settlement.

Some of the poems are epithalamiums, one of which was addressed to Domine Egidius Luyck, rector of the Latin School upon his marriage with Judith van Isendoorn. The author of the poems was Do. Selyns, the earliest poet of the province. This poem was lent to me between forty and fifty years since by the late Dr. Bruce. He died during my long absence in Europe. I have made many enquiries after it since my return, but can hear nothing of it. It was too neatly bound and too neatly written a volume to be wantonly destroyed; and I am in hopes it is still existing in the hands of some one or other of Dr. Bruce's connections." We had, however, first derived our knowledge of the former existence of the manuscript from the papers of M. du Simitiere, preserved by the Library Company of Philadelphia, which relate to a period anterior to and during the revolutionary war. Shortly after our return from Holland, the volume so long lost was placed in our hands, for such public use as we might deem proper, by Mrs. Henry E. Pierrepont of Brooklyn. It appears to have passed, on the death of Dr. Bruce,[1] into the possession of the late Peter A. Jay, Esq., the father of Mrs. Pierrepont.

---

[1] Dr. Archibald Bruce was a lineal descendant of Nicholas Bayard, the intimate friend of Selyns, and one of the witnesses to his will. The manuscript, undoubtedly, was an heir-loom in the Bayard family. Dr. Bruce conducted the American *Mineralogical Journal*, the first and only volume of which was published in 1814, and was the precursor of *Silliman's Journal*. He died in 1818.

Upon perusing the manuscript it was found to consist of about two hundred pieces of verse by Domine Selyns, composed, for the most part, in Dutch, but many of them in Latin and one in Greek, and varying in length from a single couplet to one hundred lines or more, and not averaging more than ten or twelve lines each. They consist, indeed, generally, of epitaphs, and nuptial, birth-day and other congratulatory odes, of a personal character, and were evidently intended, either, according to the practice then in great vogue, for the albums of friends, or for their private eye. The greatest number of them relate to individuals in Holland, whose memories have thus indeed been perpetuated by private friendship, but whose lives and characters have no claim upon our consideration. Such of them as relate to persons in New Netherland, and such others of the pieces in the volume, not of the character just described, as have been deemed proper, have been selected for this publication; the former for their local and personal reminiscences, the latter to show the peculiarities of his style. Some have been selected as specimens of his latinity. A few others of his poems have been added from scattered printed sources.

We are indebted to Dr. De Witt, of the Collegiate Dutch Church of New York, for the use of the original letters of Do. Selyns to the classis of Amsterdam, in preparing the brief sketch which we have been enabled to offer of the life of the author. These letters were transferred by that body a few years since to the Dutch Church at New York. Some facts in relation to his family were derived from a manuscript in his own hand-writing, submitted to our examination while at Amsterdam, by Rev. J. J. Van Voorst of that city. Dr. O'Callaghan has kindly given us the benefit of his researches made specially for the purpose in the colonial records of the state. But materials are still wanting for a satisfactory biography. Nothing has been found to illustrate his attainments in physical science to which he was disposed, though it is quite probable something for this purpose may exist among the papers of Cotton Mather, with whom he was in correspondence on that subject.

While yet engaged with the memoir and poems of Selyns, we were furnished by the Hon. Tunis G. Bergen, of New Utrecht, with some verses, also in Dutch, of another inhabitant of New Netherland, who may dispute with both Steendam and Selyns their claim, at least in point of time, to the laureate wreath of our colony. These verses were written by Nicasius de Sillè, first Councillor of State under Governor Stuyvesant. Only three of his pieces, however, have come to light, and they are to be found in the town records of New Utrecht.

Steendam, Selyns and De Sillè thus constitute the group which we have designated as the Poets of New Netherland. Others may hereafter be discovered who may be entitled to be ranked in the same class, but these three are all who are now known to us. We have been enabled to add some particulars to our former notice of Steendam, through the kindness of our learned and highly esteemed correspondents, Messrs. J. T. Bodel Nyenhuis of Leyden, and M. F. A. G. Campbell, of the Hague. Most of them are derived from an article in the *Navorscher* for 1864, by Major P. A. Lempe, late of the Dutch East India service.

The plan of this publication did not admit of inquiry as to those poets of our state who wrote in Dutch, but who did not live during the era of New Netherland; yet it may not be amiss to state that our later annals present us with the name of at least one who, born on the soil, made the language of his Batavian ancestors the medium of his inspirations. In 1802, a pamphlet was printed at Albany containing two poetical pieces by Gerrit Van Sante, of that city. They were the effusions of piety, offended by the course of the consistory of the church in regard to the employment of ministers who preached in the English language instead of the Dutch, which still maintained its hold upon the members. One of these pieces was entitled, "Een niew liedt van de onreght veerdigheydt aen de Duytse Gemeente gedaan; om gelt te heffe onnut te verbouwe en de Duytse een leeraar te outhoude schoon zy de Duytse beloovde, as sy de tweede Engelse leeraar toestonde, een Duytse leeraar te beroepe;" that is, "A new song of the

injustice done to the Dutch congregation, in raising
money uselessly to rebuild, and on withholding from
the Dutch a minister, although they promised the
Dutch, when they agreed to a second English minister, they would call a Dutch minister." The other
is on the same topic. "Een klaag liedt over de
ongevoeligheydt van de kerckraade die de Duytse
haar Godtsdienst ontneemen tegen haar beloft van,"
or, "A complaint against the insensibility of the
consistory which has deprived the Dutch of their
worship contrary to promise." Mr. Van Sante's
Dutch and his verses are neither of them perfect
models of imitation. He wrote the language as it
had been derived from the colonists, not polished
by much study. The concluding stanza of his complaint, addressing the consistory and invoking the
light of God to remove their mental blindness, and
make them love their neighbors, will suffice as a
specimen of his muse.

> "O! Kerckraadt!
> Dat Godts ryne wet ook was een ligt
> Gy sou dan uw onreght ook sien
> Hongerde gy na Godts geregligheydt
> Gy soud 'geen Godts dienst gaan verslind' en
> Als de Heer uw blindt verstandt verlight
> As Saul Jesus dan krygen in 't gesight
> Sal gy Godt en un naaste beminne."

Mr. Van Sante was over seventy years of age at
the time he wrote these poems. He died July 16,
1806, in the seventy-sixth year of his age, at Albany,
where he was born and always lived, leaving one

daughter, the wife of James Bleecker, to whose children he devised a large landed estate. He also left a character for good deeds and unostentatious acts of benevolence, more precious than his reputation as an author, though he was long afterwards not unfavorably remembered among his townsmen, at least, as the Dutch Poet.

Brooklyn,
    March 1, 1865.

MEMOIR AND POEMS

OF

JACOB STEENDAM.

Behold the contour, countenance, and outward guise,
Of STEENDAM here portrayed by Koeman's skilful hand.
His mental gifts, perused in his sweet melodies,
Provide God's Church, a harp, which does the ear enchant,
With David's heavenly song. His art who'll fully prize?
The hymning of the Lord, above all praise does rise.

JACOB STEENDAM.

Steendam was born in 1616. The place of his birth
is uncertain; though some passages in his writings
lead to the inference that it was the city of Enkhuizen
in North Holland. His parentage is also unknown.
He removed at an early age to Amsterdam, where he
continued to reside while he remained in Fatherland.
The greater part of his manhood was, however, spent
abroad, exhibiting in his career that adventurous spirit
which was the great characteristic of his countrymen
in the age when he lived. He wrote verses as a
pastime. They were generally of a lyrical character,
either amatory or psalmodic, and were accompanied
with the name of the air to which they were to be
sung. They were fugitive pieces thrown off apparently
at intervals when the more serious occupations of life
gave him leisure moments for such employment, con-
sisting for the most part of nuptial songs and congratulatory odes addressed to distinguished personages
or particular friends. They were printed from time to
time in broadsides or slips, sometimes anonymously,
at others with his name or motto, or both of them,
subscribed. He adopted the whimsical device of

noch vaster, a play upon his own name; Steendam
meaning *stone dam*, and noch vaster *still firmer*. Notwithstanding this assumption he appears to have been
a man of very unsettled purposes of life. He was for
fifteen years in the service of the West India Company[1], and in 1641, while in its employ, went to the
coast of Guinea, was at the taking of Fort Axem from
the Portuguese in February of the following year, and
remained there until 1649. Upon his return he collected his poems together and published them at
Amsterdam in a small quarto volume, in three parts,
under the title of *Den Distelvink*, the Thistle-finch or
Gold-finch. The first and second parts appeared in
1649; the third in 1650. The first part consists of love
songs and emblems; the second, of nuptial and tri-
umphal odes; and the last of spiritual songs. In the
preface to the third part he complains that a portion
of one of his poems had been stolen during his absence
and recited, as the production of another person, on
the boards of the Amsterdam theatre on New Years
day 1646, and afterwards printed among the three
prize poems of that occasion, although he had published it under his own name five years before; but as
the thief had acknowledged the larceny in the presence
of his wife, he says he will not expose his name. It

[1] "O STEENDAM! die door zoo veel zeen,
　Een reex van vijftien ronde jaeren
　U aen de Maatschappij verbint," enz.
　　　　　　PIETER VERHOEK, *Poezij*, p. 156.

was probably this circumstance that induced him to publish the Distelvink. It was a petit larceny of the smallest kind. It is curious, however, as an illustration of the early custom of New Years addresses and the scriptural spirit which the stage then admitted. The piece so written by Steendam is entitled, "A New Year's Gift dedicated to all orthodox professors of the true Christian Reformed Religion." The felony consisted in appropriating the concluding verse, as follows:

> Het nuwe-jaar dat ons leerd mijden
> Het oude quaad, en't hart besnijden:
> De slang (door 't vel) verandered haar:
> Doet soo: neemt aan den Nuwen-mensche,
> Hiertoe ik yder Lid-maat wensche
> Een eeuwig, salig Nuwe-jaer.

> The new year teaches our despising
> Old sin: our hearts a circumcising:
> Her skin the snake then changes e'er:
> So do you too: put on the New-man,
> And now I wish each Christian true man
> A new and lasting, happy year.

Many of the pieces in the Distelvink indicate the years in which they were written, though the greater portion of them have no date. The earliest year affixed to any of them is 1636. Of the character of Steendam's poetry some judgment may be formed from a perusal of the pieces hereafter reproduced, which constitute, with the Distelvink, all that we have been able to discover extant of his productions, except a few scattering verses underneath portraits and laudations prefixed to publications of some of his friends.

His machinery is usually taken from the scriptures or the classical mythology. He indulges in quaint conceits and rhymes; and evinces oftentimes a strong religious feeling. He belongs to the school of which his contemporary, Father Cats, is the great exemplar.

He went to New Netherland soon after the publication of the Distelvink, and after the termination of his employment by the West India Company, apparently with a view to a permanent settlement in the colony. In 1652 he purchased a farm at Amersfoort (Flatlands), and in the following year, a house and lot on Pearl street, and another on Broadway in New Amsterdam, and also a farm at Mespath. His name occurs in the contribution lists for the expenses of the works of defence of New Amsterdam against the Indians in 1653 and 1655,[1] as a trader: and in the latter year he was nominated, but not appointed, as an orphan master. In 1658 he applied to the Director and Council for process against a person who had overcharged him for commissions on goods sold for him. In 1660 he presented a petition, with others, to the same authorities for permission to trade to the West Coast of Africa for the purpose of importing slaves and other articles into the colony. In August of the same year he addressed a letter to the Director and Council wishing to know to whom he must apply for 190 skepels of buckwheat, being the consideration for the land at Amersfoort bought of him and reserved

---

[1] Valentine's *New York*, pp. 313 and 317.

by the company for the benefit of that town, as he was then on the eve of departure for fatherland. These recorded facts show both a fixed and continued residence by him in New Netherland during the period embraced by them, and that he was actually there in 1659, when his first poem on New Netherland was published.

He arrived in the colony at the time of great excitement concerning its boundaries, between the Dutch and English; an excitement which increased during his residence there in consequence of the continual encroachments upon the territory of the West India Company by the people of New England; the colony being in a weak state of defence, and much uneasiness on that account being felt on the part of the inhabitants. More men were wanted; and Stuyvesant, the governor, made constant appeals to the company for aid. But the truth was, the affairs of the company at home were in a bad way, and shortly after the surrender, which soon followed, of New Netherland to the English, they went into liquidation. Besides New Netherland was not a profitable colony for the company; and when, subsequently, New York was retaken by a Dutch admiral, the news was received by the reconstructed company with perfect indifference.[1] There seemed therefore neither to be the

[1] The records of the company for that period show that the intelligence of the recapture of New Amsterdam was received by the directors without even reference to a committee or any further notice whatever than a minute of the fact.

means nor the disposition to relieve the colonists. On
the other hand the Dutch government had no charge
over the colony, as it was merely a commercial post of
the company, which had been erected while the independence of the Dutch provinces was yet unacknow-
ledged by the Spanish monarch, and as a means of
annoyance to his commerce. Having accomplished
the purposes of the state policy in which it originated,
its further career did not interest the government in
any special degree; and least of all could the colonies
demand its assistance. The people who had settled in
New Netherland were thus thrown upon their own
resources and expedients in a great measure. They
fortified New Amsterdam by levies or contributions of
their own. Descriptions, showing the advantages of
the country for settlement, were written and sent to
Holland for publication in order to invite immigration.
Steendam, too, invoked his muse in the cause, and in
1659 sent over his first effort in its behalf, in a short
poem which he called *The Complaint of New Amsterdam to her Mother;* in which New Amsterdam, per-
sonified as the daughter of the old city of Amsterdam, represents that she was born in time of war, but
had been deserted by her mother and left to the kindness of her sponsors; that she had, notwithstanding
the maternal neglect, grown up a handsome person,
with a rich property, the envy of her neighbors, whose
swine were turned in upon it. She asks for laborers
to till her lands. Under this guise the circumstances

of the erection of the West India Company (the sponsors) and the encroachments of the English (the swine)
are described. This poem is the first attempt, of
which we have any knowledge, in verse in the colony;
and both for its priority in that respect and as an historical piece exhibiting the feelings and temper of the
colonists at an alarming time, it claims a greater
degree of attention than its poetical merits simply
would entitle it to demand. Hence, measured by the
standard and accorded the privileges which have been
adjudged Sandys, the first poet of Virginia, and Mor-
rell the first poet of New England, Steendam is hereafter to rank as the first poet of New York. The
Complaint of New Amsterdam was followed, in 1661,
by another poem from his muse in the form of a
panegyric upon New Netherland, portraying its excellencies and advantages for settlement in no sparing
colors. It was entitled *The Praise of New Netherland*,
and was published in that year in a small quarto
form. It is an elaborate description of the natural
productions of the land, and bears strong internal evidence, both in its language and ideas, of Steendam's
personal residence in the country; but it is not certain
that it was either written in the colony or published
while he was there. In fact such evidence as we
possess points to the contrary. The declining condition of the West India Company had compelled its
directors several years before this period to dispose of
a portion of their territory on the South River, or

Delaware, to the city of Amsterdam, which had undertaken to colonize it, but as yet with little success. In 1662 a renewed effort for that purpose was made by the burgomasters of the city. A community of persons known as Mennonites was organized for the purpose of settlement on the Delaware. The leader of this enterprise was Peter Cornelisen Plockhoy of Zierikzee in Zeeland, who published in the last mentioned year a pamphlet with the title: "Short and clear plan, serving as a mutual contract to lighten the labor, anxiety and trouble of all kinds of handicraftsmen by the establishment of a community or colony on the South River in New Netherland, comprising agriculturalists, seafaring persons, all kinds of necessary trades-people and masters of good arts and sciences, under the protection of Their High Mightinesses, the Lords States General of the United Netherlands, and particularly under the favorable auspices of the Honorable Magistrates of the city of Amsterdam, etc."[1] This high-sounding publication was intended to invite associates to engage in the scheme,

---

[1] *Kort en klaer ontwerp*, te Amst. 1662, small 4to, 16 pages. This collection consists of 1. the agreement between Plockhoy and the city of Amsterdam, and may be found in N. Y. Colonial Documents collected by Mr. Broadhead and translated by Dr. O'Callaghan, II, p. 176. 2. A sonnet by Karel ver Loove upon the maxim, *Eendraght maeckt magt*, Union makes strength. 3. The plan of association. 4. Spurring-verses by Jacob Steendam; and 5. A notice that those who intend to join the association must be ready to embark by the middle of September, &c., &c. This publication of Plockhoy preceded by a few months that of the *Kort Verhael van Nieuw Nederlants*, which, although it appeared without the name either of author or printer, evidently emanated from a similar source.

and contains at the end a number of stanzas by Steendam, entitled *Prickel-Vaersen*, that is, spurring-verses,
or lines to urge or spur on the friends of the under-
taking. In this piece, which, as will be seen, is a
generalization of what the poet had already written in
the praise of New Netherland, he speaks of his personal knowledge of the country. As the agreement
between Plockhoy and the city of Amsterdam was
dated in June 1662, and the colonists were to sail in
September, which was probably some time after the
publication of the pamphlet, as that was intended to
be circulated for the purpose of obtaining more associates, it is almost beyond question that Steendam was
in Amsterdam at the time the pamphlet appeared; and
if so, he may have been there on the publication of
the praise of New Netherland in the preceding year.
He certainly had left the colony in 1663, as we find a
minute in the records of April in that year, of a petition presented to the director and council by *attorney*,
in his name, for leave to fence in his land at Mespath
Kil. But his retaining the ownership of that property leads us to believe that though he had gone to
Holland he had not abandoned his residence in the
colony, but intended to return. The interest which he
seems to have taken in promoting emigration from
Holland to the colony at this period, as shown by *The
Praise of New Netherland*, and the stanzas in Plockhoy's book, adds strength to this conclusion. But he
did not return to New Netherland. The storm which

had been so long gathering over the heads of the colonists was now ready to burst, and in the following
year the English took possession of the colony in the
name of the Duke of York. Then Steendam gave up
the country which he had sought to save from its
impending fate; and true to that law of his nature
which led him ever to seek his fortune beyond the
seas, he embarked from Amsterdam in 1665 for the
East Indies.[1] Few traces of him occur after this
period, but such as are found show that he was at
Batavia. There is a fine portrait of Cornelius Speel-
man, engraved by A. Blooteling and dated Batavia, 10
December 1670, with a stanza of six lines signed
Jacob Steendam, *noch vaster*. A manuscript memo-
randum on the portrait of Steendam, in possession of
Mr. Müller, states that in 1671 he was *vader* or superin-
tendent of the Orphan House at Batavia. This is the
last mention of him which we have seen: and we are
therefore as much at a loss to know where he ended
his days as where he began them. We may perhaps
reasonably infer that he died in the East. There may
be memorials of him in existence at Batavia; and we
may hereafter learn the particulars of his life subsequent to his arrival there, and of his death. He may
have descendants living there, for he was married, as
we have already seen in his statement that the confession of the thief who stole his poetry was made in

---

[1] Van der Aa's supplement to P. G. Witsen Geysbeek's *Dictionary
of Dutch Poets*, III, 202.

presence of his wife. Her name was Sara de Ross-
chou;[1] and he has addressed to her, in the Distelvink,
an ode which he devotes to her religious character
alone. There are, doubtless, too, more facts in regard
to him yet to be found in Holland; and we have reason to believe he published other poems than those
we have mentioned; his spirit was too active to leave
either mind or body long at rest. [2]

---

[1]In the records of the Dutch Church of New Amsterdam, of members of that church, the entry as to Steendam and his wife reads;
" Jacob Steendam and Sarah *Abrahams* his wife," and in the margin
" left for the East Indies."

[2] We have to some extent realized from the sources stated in the
introduction, since this was written, the expectations here expressed in
regard to information from Batavia. It appears from Major Lempe's
investigations that Steendam was a man of fervid piety, and was
accepted by the Amsterdam Chamber of the East India Company as
visitor and consoler of the sick, for the classis of Amsterdam, in
Batavia. This service was an inferior ministerial office in the Dutch
Reformed church for the purposes which the name denotes, and not
entitling the incumbent to preach. He sailed from Holland on this
mission in the ship Rising Sun on the 9th of April, 1666, and reached
Batavia, in the island of Java on the 18th of October, following. Upon
his own request he was sent in the following year by the consistory
of Batavia to Bengal ; and, in expectation of his return thence, which
took place in January 1668, he was in his absence chosen governor of
the Orphans House at Batavia. His wife was at the same time
installed governess of the establishment, and subsequently, upon his
death, took the sole charge of it. When exactly he died does not yet
appear, but it seems her death occurred in 1673, as in September of
that year their daughter, Vredegund Steendam, and her betrothed
husband, Cornelius Wadde of Ooltgensplaat, near Brielle in South
Holland, schoolmaster of the Orphans House, were designated by
the authorities of Batavia to succeed her mother, who was in charge
of the institution as survivor of her husband, and was then just
deceased.

Mr. Campbell, the accomplished assistant librarian of the Royal
Library at the Hague, gives us the title of another work of Steendam, printed at Batavia in 1671, in 8 vo., viz. ZEEDE-ZANGEN VOOR

Steendam enjoyed the esteem of distinguished contemporaries. Peter Verhoek addressed two poems to him on his departure for Batavia, evincing much feeling and expressed with elegance. The few lines of Johan Nieuhoff, underneath his portrait, are terse and neat, and testify to the religious character of his poems. As we have there given a translation, we may here present a copy of them in their original dress. They are as follows:

> " Hier Ziet gij d'Ommetrek, het Aanschijn, en het weezen,
>   Van STEENDAM; door de hand van Kooman afgebeeld.
> De Gaaven van Zyn Geest, in Maatzang uitgeleezen,
>   Verstrecken Godts Gemeent, een Harp, die d' Ooren streeld,
> Met Davidts Hemel-taal. Wie kan zijn kunst vol-looven?
> Des Heeren Lofgezang, gaat alle Loff te booven.
>
> JOHAN NIEUHOFF."

Nieuhoff is well known as the author of two works contained in the collection of Montanus, one relating to Brazil, and the other to the embassy of the Dutch East India Company to the Great Cham of Tartary in 1655-7. It was probably at Batavia that he became acquainted with our poet. Both these testimonials go perhaps more to Steendam's personal worth than to his excellence as a poet. As such we may accept them in behalf of a land far away from his natal home, and probable final resting place, but where he was first to strike the lyre which has since been touched by many more brilliant and more fortunate hands.

DE BATAVISCHE JONKHEYT, *Moral Songs for the Batavian Youth.* Some lines by him are also to be found prefixed to Nieuhoff's *Zee en Lant Reise doer Oost-Indie*, August 1681, returning as it were the compliment by that author on the portrait of Steendam. They bear date at Batavia, 24 Oct. 1670.

POEMS.

KLAGT

NIEUW·AMSTERDAM.

'k Ben een *Na-nicht* van de Goden
Die an *d' Amstel* haar geboden
Stellen, tot een vaste baak:
Tot een huel, en tot een wraak.

   'k Ben uit *Amsterdam* geboren:
'k Heb haar borsten vroeg verloren;
Want men heeft my strak gespeend:
't Geen ik dikwils heb beweend.

   'k Heb veel ongemak geleden,
'k Heb van jongs-op-an gestreden:
Want doen ik ter wereld kwam,
'k Onheil zijn begindsel nam.

   Dunkt u dit een seldsaam wonder?
Mijn geboorte in 't bysonder:
Met diens toeval, daar omtrent,
Maakt u dese saak bekend.

   Wilt gy na mijn afkomst vragen?
'k Ben een langen tijdt gedragen,
In de lendenen van *Mars:*
't Scheen, mijn Moeder wierd my wars.

THE COMPLAINT

OF

NEW AMSTERDAM.

I'm a grandchild of the Gods
Who on th' Amstel have abodes;
Whence their orders forth are sent
Swift for aid and punishment.
    I, of Amsterdam, was born,
Early of her breasts forlorn;
From her care so quickly weaned
Oft have I my fate bemoaned.
    From my youth up left alone,
Naught save hardship have I known;
Dangers have beset my way
From the first I saw the day.
    Think you that a cause for marvel?
This will then the thread unravel,
And the circumstances trace,
Which upon my birth took place.
    Would you ask for my descent?
Long the time was it I spent
In the loins of warlike Mars.
'T seems my mother, seized with fears,

Tot een misval, van verschrikken:
Doch ik sal niet licht verklikken,
Hoe de saak is toe-gegaan.
Siet: ik heb wel eer verstaan,
   Dat ook *Bacchus* ('t zijn geen dromen)
Soo is voor den dagh gekomen
Uyt de Dyè van Jupiter.
Maar mijn reden gaan te verr'.

'k Mach mijn eygen saak verhalen,
Om niet van den wegh te dwalen:
Schoon ook *Bacchus* my (als vriend)
In mijn saken, vaardig diend.

   't Vroed-wijf dat my heeft ontfangen,
Was Bellone: die een langen
Tijd, geseten heeft, met smart:
Want den arbeid viel te hart.

Mijn geboorte was met tranen:
Midts mijn Buuren, d' Indianen
My vervolgden, nacht en dach:
Wijl ik nau mijn *Moeder* sach.

   Doch mijn *Voogden*, en mijn *Peters*,
Die verschaften my wat beters:
Want sy vochten voor mijn lijf,
En bestelden my een Wijf,

   Tot een Voedster, die haar borsten
Niet verschoonde, als my dorsten:
Dit was *Ceres:* die my heeft
Op-gequeeckt, van 't geen sy geeft.
   'k Wil haar (boven allen) prijsen:

Prematurely brought me forth.
But I now am very loth
To inform how this befel;
Though 'twas thus, I know full well.

Bacchus, too,—it is no dream,—
First beheld the daylight's beam
From the thigh of Jupiter.
But my reasons go too far.

My own matter must I say,
And not loiter by the way,
E'en though Bacchus oft has proven
Friend to me in my misfortune.

Now the mid-wife who received me,
Was Bellona; in suspense, she
Long did sit in trembling fear,
For the travail was severe.

From the moment I was born,
Indian neighbors made me mourn.
They pursued me night and day,
While my mother kept away.

But my sponsors did supply
Better my necessity;
They sustained my feeble life;
They procured a bounteous wife

As my nurse, who did not spare
To my lips her paps to bare.
This was Ceres; freely she
Rendered what has nurtured me.

Her most dearly will I prize;

Want sy deed' mijn hoornen rijsen,
Dat ik wies van tijd, tot tijd,
Midden in mijn last, en strijd.

Doch ik wil hier dit byvoegen,
'k Heb my dikwils laten noegen
Met Sappaan, en Harte-vleysch:
Schraal, en nauwlijks na den eysch.

Als ik dus begon te wassen,
Scheen ik nergens op te passen:
Siet, mijn borsten wierden net,
En mijn heupe vast geset.

Self *Nephtuni* wierd my gonstig:
Ja *Mercuri* gau, en konstig,
Kleeden my, met Goud, en Sy:
Dies scheen elk het vryen vry.

Maar men poogde my te schaken.
Om het blosen van mijn kaken:
Om de schoonheyd van mijn jeugd:
Als een voorwerp, an de vreugd.

Om de vruchten van mijn Bogert.
Seeker, 't is een droge-drogert,
Die een Vrijster (soo begoedt)
Niet te meerder anstoot doet.

Want ik sou wel durven roemen,
Dat men niemand weet te noemen,
Die een beter plaats besit:
Als die ik heb tot mijn wit.

She has made my horns to rise;
Trained my growth through tender years,
'Midst my burdens and my cares.

   True, both simple 'twas and scant,
What I had to feed my want.
Oft 't was nought except Supawn [1]
And the flesh of buck or fawn.

   When I thus began to grow,
No more care did they bestow.
Yet my breasts are full and neat,
And my hips are firmly set.

   Neptune shows me his good will;
Merc'ry, quick, exerts his skill
Me t'adorn with silk and gold;
Whence I'm sought by suitors bold.

   Stricken by my cheek's fresh bloom,
By my beauteous youthful form,
They attempt to seize the treasure
To enjoy their wanton pleasure.

   They, my orchards too, would plunder.
Truly 'tis a special wonder,
That a maid, with such a portion,
Does not suffer more misfortune :

   For, I venture to proclaim,
No one can a maiden name,
Who with richer land is blessed
Than th' estate by me possessed.

---

[1] A pure Indian word, adopted by the colonists and still in use,
meaning mush or boiled meal of maize.

Siet, mijn tuyn leyd an twee stromen
Die van 't Oost, en 't Noorden komen,
En haar storten in de Zee:
Visch-rijk boven allen mee.

Melk, en Boter, Ooft, en Fruyten,
Dat men nau 't getal kan uyten:
Tuyn-vrucht, wat men wenschen mach:
Granen 't beste dat men sach.

Alles wat men kan bedenken,
Komt den Rijken-gever schenken,
(Neffens een gesonde lucht)
An mijn jonkheydt seer beducht:

Om de Swijen, die met voeten
Mijn gewas vertreen, en wroeten
Al mijn rijke Akkers om:
Schoon ik hou my stil, als stom:

Met een hoope, op mijn Moeder:
Die my, kan een trouwe hoeder
Strekken, in dit ongeval:
't Is mijn wensch, en 't isset al.

So ik maar mach Bouw-liën krijgen,
'k Sal niet voor de Groten swijgen:
Want mijn werk-volk is te min,
Krijg ik maar een groot gesin,

'k Sal mijn Moeders keuken vullen,
Met mijn leuren, met mijn prullen:
Met mijn Bont, Toebak, en Graan:
Dat sy Pruyssen sal versmaân.

JACOB STEENDAM,
Noch vaster.

See! two streams my garden bind,
From the East and North they wind,—
Rivers pouring in the sea,
Rich in fish, beyond degree.

Milk and butter; fruits to eat
No one can enumerate;
Ev'ry vegetable known;
Grain the best that e'er was grown.

All the blessings man e'er knew,
Here does our Great Giver strew,
(And a climate ne'er more pure)
But for me,—yet immature,

Fraught with danger; for the Swine
Trample down these crops of mine;
Up-root, too, my choicest land;
Still and dumb, the while, I stand,

In the hope, my mother's arm
Will protect me from the harm.
She can succour my distress.
Now my wish, my sole request,—

Is for men to till my land;
So I'll not in silence stand.
I have lab'rors almost none;
Let my household large become;

I'll my mother's kitchen furnish
With my knicknacks, with my surplus;
With tobacco, furs and grain;
So that Prussia she'll disdain.

JACOB STEENDAM,
Noch vaster.

'T LOF

VAN

NUW-NEDERLAND

DAARIN, KORT, EN GRONDIG WORD ANGEWESEN D'UYTMUN-
TENDE HOEDANIGHEDEN, DIE HET HEEFT IN DE SUY-
VERHEYT DES LUCHTS VRUCHTBAARHEYT DES
AARDRIJKS, VOORT-TELING DES VEES, OVER-
VLOED DES WILDS, EN VISSCHEN: MET
DE WELGELEGENHEYT TOT SCHIP-
VAARD, EN KOOPHANDEL.

THE PRAISE

OF

NEW NETHERLAND.

WHEREIN ARE BRIEFLY AND TRULY SHOWN THE EXCELLENT
QUALITIES WHICH IT POSSESSES IN THE PURITY OF
THE AIR, FERTILITY OF THE SOIL, PRODUCTION OF
THE CATTLE, ABUNDANCE OF GAME AND FISH:
WITH ITS ADVANTAGES FOR NAVIGATION
AND COMMERCE.

'T

LOF VAN NUW-NEDERLAND.

GE-EYGENED

DE ACHTBARE HEERE CORNELIS VAN RUYVEN:

RAAD EN GEHEYMSCHRYVER VAN DE E. WEST-

INDISCHE MAAT-SCHAP: ALDAAR,

Getrouwe, en seer op-rechte, Voorstander
van Nuw-Nederland.

------ ◆◆◆ ------

Een ander, scherpt zijn schaft, en gau vernuft
Op d'ydelheyt van lof, en roem en suft
In 't Doolhof der Gedachten: die (verbluft)
In 't duyster dolen.

Op 't voorwerp van 't geen smaad, of niet behoord
Daar eygen eer (in yder konstig woord)
Behartigd word: en vlugge sinnen smoord
In donk're holen.

Voor my, Ik kies een ander hoger-kant.
Mijn *Sang-Heldin* verheft Nuw-Nederland:
Daar 't *Amstels*-Volk haar Volk'ren heeft geplant,
Gequeekt tot heden.

Nuw-Nederland, gy edelste Gewest
Daar d'Opperheer (op 't heerlijkst) heeft gevest
De Volheyt van zijn gaven: alder-best:
In alle Leden.

THE

PRAISE OF NEW NETHERLAND.

DEDICATED TO

THE HONORABLE CORNELIS VAN RUYVEN:

COUNSELLOR AND SECRETARY OF THE ·HON. WEST

INDIA COMPANY THERE,

Faithful and very upright Promoter
of New Netherland.

With sharpened pen and wit, one tunes his lays,
To sing the vanity of fame and praise:
His moping thoughts, bewildered in a maze,
    In darkness wander.
What brings disgrace, what constitutes a wrong,
These form the burden of the tuneful song:
And honor saved, his senses then among
    The dark holes ponder.
For me, it is a nobler theme I sing.
New Netherland springs forth my heroine;
Where Amstel's folk did erst their people bring,
    And still they flourish.
New Netherland, thou noblest spot of earth,
Where bounteous Heaven ever poureth forth
The fulness of HIS gifts, of greatest worth,
    Mankind to nourish.

Wie, (buiten gonst, of onwil) u beseft
En kundig, uw hoedanigheden treft
Sal billyken, die u verheffing heft
     Tot aan de wolken.
So hy, de vier Hoofd-stoffen in u peyld:
En op het loot van kennis, die beseyld
En krust: en in sijn oordeel niet en feyld
     Voor vrije volken.
Uw *Lucht*, en dun, en helder, sijn, en klaar,
Doordringende: gematigd nochtand daar
Den Westen, en Noord-westen wind: die haar
     Van dampen leedigd.
Van damp, en mist, en nevelachtigheyt;
Von stank, die uyt de Poelen sich verspreyd
Om-hoog, in strijd; en vlugtig voor haar scheyd
     En 't weer bevredigd
Soo dat geen Pest, noch Lazery u plaagd;
Die 't eene Land, het ander over-draagd:
Ten waar, u volk bysonder wierd belaagd
     Van grove sonden.
Uw Son, des *Vuurs* oorspronkelyke-gloed
En warremte: en 't voedsel hat het voed,
Is suyver, heet, en (op het eelste) goed;
     Vol sap bevonden.
't En is geen Turf, geen koe mest (uytgedroogd)
Geen koolen, die de nood (tot nut) beoogd:
Geen plaggen, van de heyde op-gehoogd,
     Tot brand geheven,

Whoe'er to you a judgment fair applies,
And knowing, comprehends your qualities,
Will justify the man who, to the skies,
    Extols your glories.
Who studies well your natural elements,
And with the plumb of science, gains a sense
Of all the four: fails not in their defence,
    Before free juries.
Your *Air*, so clear, so sharp to penetrate,
The Western breezes softly moderate;
And tempering the heat, they separate
    It from all moisture.
From damp, and mist, and fog, they set it free;
From smells of pools, they give it liberty:
The struggling stenches made to mount on high,
    And be at peace there.
No deadly pest its purity assails,
To spread infection o'er your hills and vales,
Save when a guilty race, great sins bewails
    In expiating.
Your Sun, th' original of *Fire* and heat,
The common nutriment of both to eat,
Is warm and pure; in plants most delicate,
    Much sap creating.
Nor turf, nor dried manure,[1]—within your doors,
Nor coal, extracted from earth's secret stores;
Nor sods, uplifted from the barren moors,
    For fuel given;

---

[1] This article is used in some parts of the Netherlands for fuel.

Dat 's Menschen hoofd, en breyn bedwelmen kan,
Door quaden reuk, en bangen-lucht; Waarvan
Een kloek verstand (in meenig geestig Man)
　　　　　Word uyt-gedreven.
Het ruyme bosch, verschaft u beter brand;
't Is Noten-hout, dat niemand heeft geplant
Dat haart, en huys (voor felle winters) mand,
　　　　—Als dap're helden.
Met vettigheyt, en scherpigheyt, ver-rijkt.
Wiens heete-vlam, geen vocht, noch koude wijkt.
Wiens geur, en reuk (vol angenaamheyt) lijkt
　　　　　Na *Edens* velden.
Uw *Water* (varsch, en klaar, en koel, en soet)
Dat uyt de grond (met dub'le overvloed)
Gedurig vloeyt, tot alle plaatsen; doet
　　　　　Veel beeken vloeijen.
Tot laafenis van 't Wild, en 't Tamme-vee:
Tot wasdom van 't gewas, op yder stee:
Verquikking van de Menschen, die hier mêe
　　　　　Voorspoedig groeijen.
Uw *Aarde* (seer verscheiden, in den aart)
Is swart, en wit, en rood, en blau; en baard
Uyt haren schoot, een ryken oogst; en spaard
　　　　　Al wat de mond vleyd.
So veelderiev. dat het nau eynde heeft.
En voerd (vol-op) al wat door adem leefd;
't Geen sy, weêrom tot spijs des Menschen geeft,
　　　　　En syn geshondheyt.

Which, with foul stench the brain intoxicate;
And thus, by fetid gas which they create,
The intellects of many, wise and great,
                    Men are out-driven.
The forests do, with better means, supply
The hearth and house: the stately hickory,
Not planted, does the winter fell defy, —
                    A valiant warden;
So closely grained, so rich with fragrant oil,
Before its blaze both wet and cold recoil;
And sweetest perfumes float around the while,
                    Like 'n Eden's garden.
The *Water* clear and fresh, and pure and sweet,
Springs up continually beneath the feet,
And every where the gushing fountains meet,
                    In brooks o'erflowing,
Which animals refresh, both tame and wild;
And plants conduce to grow on hill and field;
And these to man unnumbered comforts yield,
                    And quickly growing.
The *Earth* in soils of different shades appears,
Black, blue and white, and red; its bosom bears
Abundant harvests; and, what pleases, spares
                    Not to surrender.
No bounds exist to their variety.
They nourishment afford most plenteously
To creatures which, in turn, man's wants supply
                    And health engender.

O vrucht-rijk *Land*, vol zeegens, opgehoopt;
Wie in 't vernuft, uw gaven over-loopt;
En yder deel, ten rechten-eynde noopt,
    Die sal bespeuren,
Dat gy, geheel (in allen zijt volmaakt;
Indien oyt Land volmaaktheyt heeft geraakt.
Ontdankbaar is hy dan, die u oyt laakt;
    Of vuyl sou keuren.
Uw *Sit-plaats* is d'Amerikaansche-kust
In 't Noorder-deel. Daar aller Sinnne-lust
Versadigd word : Ja rykelijk geblust.
    Gy hebt vermogen
Te geven, al wat eenig Volk behoefd,
Tot nooddruft: En verheuging, die bedroefd
Verquikking eyscht. Of sich in wellust toeft :
    Voor aller oogen.
De groote *Zee* bespoeld uw voorste-strand;
Die (als een dijk) zich voor u Velden kant:
Door-aderd, met veel killen : die het *Land*,
    En 't Bosch verfrisschen.
Die van 't gebergt, en heuvels neder-vliên :
En 't Molen-werk, bequame plaatsen biên
Op d'oevers van u stromen. Waard te sien :
    Gepropt met Visschen.
En Prik, en Aal, en Sonne-vis, en Baars :
Die (blank en geel) u Taaff'len als wat raars)
Vercieren kan : ook Elft, en Twalft niet schaars,
    Maar overvloedig.

O fruitful land ! heaped up with blessings kind,
Whoe'er your several virtues brings to mind,—
Its proper value to each gift assigned,
                    Will soon discover,
If ever land perfection have attained,
That you in all things have that glory gained;
Ungrateful mortal, who, your worth disdained,
                    Would pass you over.
In North America, behold your *Seat*,
Where all that heart can wish you satiate,
And where oppressed with wealth inordinate,
                    You have the power,
To bless the people with whate'er they need;
The melancholy, from their sorrows, lead;
The light of heart, exulting pleasure cede,
                    Who never cower.
The *Ocean* laves secure the outer shore,
Which, like a dyke, is raised your fields before;
And streams, like arteries, all veined o'er,
                    The woods refreshing;
And rolling down from mountains and the hills,
Afford, upon their banks, fit sites for mills;
And furnish, what the heart with transport fills,
                    The finest fishing.
The lamprey, eel and sunfish, and the white
And yellow perch, which grace your covers dight;
And shad and striped bass, not scarce, but quite
                    Innumerable.

Steenbrassem, Steur, en Dartien, en Knor-haan,[1]
En Zee-baars, die geen Vorst sal laten slaan:
En Kabellau: en Salm die (wel gebraan)

     Is vet, en voedig.

Swart-vis, en Roch, en Haring, en Makreel,
Schelvis, Masbank, en Voreu die (se veel)
Tot walgens toe, de Netten vuld: en heel

     Min word ge-eeten.

So gaat het hier: dat 's Werelts overvloed,
(Waar meê de Mensch, word koninglijk gevoed
Door gulle gunst des milden gevers) doet

     Hem vaak vergeeten.

Weekvis, en Schol, en Carper, Bot, en Snoek.
Ja gy en hebt geen poel; geen water-hoek,
Of 't krielter vol van Visschen: die (te soek)

     Licht zijn te vinden.

En Kreeft, en Krab, en Mossels: Oesters, die
Een, beter is als in EUROPA drie
In veelheyt heel on-kenbaar, voor hem, wie

     't Mocht onderwinden.

De Schild-pad, en de Zee-hond, en den Hay,
De Walvis, en Tonjin speeld in u Bay:
En toond Gods macht, en wonderheden. Fray

     Om an te merken.

De seldsaamheên in 't Banelose diep:
De diepte, van de *Wijsheyt*, die het schiep:

---

[1] The *knorhaan*, belonging to a species called by the English, after the French, *gurnard* or *gurnet*, is caught on the coast of England in large quantities by the Dutch fishermen. It is a small bony fish, not much esteemed. It does not exist in America. The poet refers,

The bream and sturgeon, drumfish and gurnard;
The sea-bass which a prince would not discard;
The cod and salmon,—cooked with due regard,
                    Most palatable.
The black, and rock-fish, herring, mackerel,
The haddock, mosbankers and roach which fill
The nets to loathing; and so many, all
                    Cannot be eaten.
And thus it happens here, that in the flood
Which, rolling from the Fountain of all Good,
O'erwhelms weak mortal man with royal food,
                    He is forgotten.
You've weak-fish, carp, and turbot; pike and plaice;
There's not a pool or tiny water trace,
Where swarm not myriads of the finny race,
                    Easily taken.
Crabs, lobsters, mussels; oysters, too, there be
So large, that one does overbalance three
Of those of Europe; and, in quantity,
                    No one can reckon.
The tortoise, seal and shark; and in your bay,
The mighty whale and porpoise sporting, they
The power and wondrous works of God display
                    For our beholding.
And curious forms come out the shoalless deep,
Whose depths produced by Wisdom Infinite,

---

probably, to the *porgy* of our shores. *Twaalf* and *dertien* (striped bass
and drumfish) mentioned in this and the preceding stanza, are
Dutch colonial names, unknown in Holland, as the fish are peculiar
to the American waters.

Die noyt en slaapt, noch nimmermeer en sliep:

     Maar werkt, in 't werken.

Het wild Gedeirt' dat door de Bosschen rend

By duysenden: en nau sijn Meester kend:

Word (als een Lam) tot 's Menschen nut gewend:

     En vlees, en vellen.

De Bever, en den Otter, schoon van bont.

De Visscher, die nau sijns gelijk en vond:

De Katalos (voor oude-Leên) gesond

     Die Gichten quellen.

Den Espan, en de Vos, de Mink, en Haas,

De Mater, en Eenkhooren: die de baas

In 't vluchten speeld: en nochtans is het aas

     Van grage monden:

Van Leeuw,[1] en Beer, en Wolf, en ander Wild:

Dat (in de Jaeht) sijn ruyme-tijd verspild:

Tot dat de maag, en honger is gestild:

     De proy verslonden.

Den Eland, en de Hinde, en het Hart

Dat (vluchtende) sich dickwijls vind verward

In 't Bosch: wanneer hy 't met de laatste smart

     Moet duur bekopen.

't *Gevogelte* dat sich tot Roven sneld:

En kleynder soort, steeds (als vervolger) queld,

Is d'Arend, en de Valk, die 't blauwe-veld

     Met 't oog door-lopen.

---

[1] It is difficult to say what animal is here meant. Van der Donk and Dominie Megapolensis, whose descriptions of the production of the country are the most accurate given by the early writers, both also speak of lions existing there; but the animal generally known

Have never slept and never more will sleep,
His works unfolding.

The *Animals* which in the woods roam free
By thousands, and are no one's property,
Are reared like lambs, their flesh and skins to be
For man's sustaining.

The beaver, and the otter, clean of limb;
The weasel, which has scarce the like of him;
The wild cat, strengthening the old, who seem,
With gout complaining.

Raccoon and fox, with marten, mink and hare;
The nimble squirrels, leaping through the air
And flying; which, to craving stomachs, are
Baits most decoying.

Bears, lions, wolves and other beasts of prey,
The chase has long since made to waste away,
Their maws, with naught the hunger to allay,
Themselves destroying.

The elk, the hind and hart which, fleeing, bound
Far in the forest depths, and there are found;
And when at last they feel the fatal wound,
Die hard and crying.

Of *Birds*, there is a knavish robbing crew,
Which constantly the smaller tribes pursue;
The hawk and eagle swoop the azure blue,
With sharp eyes prying.

---

as such never has been found in New Netherland. The wild cat, which some have conjectured to be referred to, is expressly mentioned in one of the preceding stanzas as a distinct species. The poet confesses he had never seen lions himself, when he says they had all been killed off.

De Kuyken-dief, de Havik, (fel van klau)
De Sperwer, en Steen-kryter, die soo gau
Ontdekken kan sijn vyand: als hy flau
　　　　　Is in het vlieden.
De End, de Gans, Kalkoen, en Troste-swaan,
De Duyker, en de Reyger, en de Kraan,
De Snep, en Wulp, en Meerle, en Berk-haan:
　　　　　Staan voor 't gebiedeen.
De Duyf, Patrys, Fasant, and Majijs dief;
De Smient (die self een lek're-tong verhief)
De Taling, en de Lijster: tot gerief
　　　　　En dienst des Menschen.
't Getal, 't geslacht, de soorten altemaal
Der Vogelen, zijn buyten kun, en taal
't Was dan gewis, een nodeloos-verhaal,
　　　　　Haar kun te wenschen.
Het Bosch, t Gebergt, de laagt, en 't vlakke-veld
Is (uyt den aard) so rykelijk besteld,
Met meenigte van *Vruchten:* Die het teld
　　　　　Sal 't al niet treffen.
De Akers zijn en bitter, en weer soet:
De Noten (seer verscheyden) dubbel goed:
Kastanjen die ik (boven and're moet)
　　　　　En sal, verheffen.
d'Aard-bes pronkt, met een rood-schaarlaken kleur:
De Pruym, en Kars, en Druyf (vol soete geur)
D'aard-akers, ee Aard-boonjes, zijn te keur:
　　　　　En Aartisokken.
De Kruys, de Moer; de Clau, en Swarte-bey,

The chicken saker-hawk, with talons fell;
The sparrow-hawk; the vigilant castrel
Watching his enemy till he may reel
               And faint in flying.
The duck, the goose, the turkey, and proud swan,
The diver and the heron and the crane,
The snipe, the curlew, merlin and moorhen,
               The foremost vieing;
The dove and pheasant, thievish blackbird, quail;
The widgeon, which an epicure may hail;
The teal and bob-o'-lincoln, all avail
               For man's enjoyment.
But names are wanting wholly to explain
The numerous species of the feathered train;
And surely the recital were a vain,
               Misspent employment.
The hills and valleys, fields and forests wide,
As richly are, by nature's hand, supplied
With *Fruits.* Of which all will be satisfied
               By this true story.
Acorns there are, the bitter and the sweet;
And nuts of various kinds, all choice to eat;
Of these the chestnuts, with the rest compete
               And win the glory.
And strawberries, which in proud scarlet shine;
The plum, the cherry, and grape clustering vine;
The ground-nut and the ground-bean, both we find;
               The artichoke, too.
The gooseberry, both sorts of mulberries;

Knof-look, en Look, en Vette-kous, en Prey,
De Hop, en Muut schynd (met een soet gevley)
Het oog te lokken.
Uw Bosch schaft Hout tot Huys, en Schip, en Schuyt.
En Bies, en Riet, en Hoy, en ruijgte, spruyt
(In overvloed) ten gullen Aard-rijk uyt.
Uw Strand geeft steenen.
Tot allerley gebruyk, seer nut, te saam:
Tot malen, en tot slypen heel bequaam:
Tot-Metsel-werk, en Straat. 't Geen nau de naam
Is te verleenen.
Quick-silver, Goud,[1] en Pot-loot, en Kristal,
Vol-aarde, en Pot-aarde. 't Is 'er al,
Wat oyt vernuft (met konst) bedenken sal:
Of kan versinnen.
Het Heel-*Kruyd*, en Genees-Kruyd (veel geacht)
Dat wonderlijk, en met een groote-kracht,
Genesen kan de quetsing: en d'on-macht,
En siekt, van binnen.
De Maselyn: en 't geurig Salsefras,
Dat als kannnel een flauwe Ziel genas,
Is daar geacht (als onkruyt) een gewas
Om uyt te roeijen.
So staat het Kruyd, by duysenden op 't Land
Op 't hoog gebergt, en an de Water-kant.
In werking vreemt, en boven ons verstand:
Schoon 't mogt ons moeijen.

---

[1] The belief in the existence of gold was universal among the colonists, and specimens of rock containing it, as was supposed, were sent to Holland, at different times, for analyzation. The

The garlick, leek and field-salad and cives;
And hops and mints, with sweetest flatteries,
                    The eyes provoke do.
Within your woods, for house and ship, is found
Good building timber; in your untilled ground,
Do reeds and rushes and wild grass abound;
                    Upon your border
Lie stone for every use; some suitable
For polishing and grinding; some as well
For masonry and streets. 'Tis hard to tell
                    Them all in order.
Blacklead and chrystal, quicksilver and gold;
And clay to full or bake; your hills unfold
Whatever art and science seek to mould,
                    Or can discover.
You've *herbs*, both wholesome and medicinal,
Possessed of virtues wondrous powerful
The failing strength to raise, and wounds to heal,
                    And curing fever.
Sweet marjoram; and sassafras, whose root,
Like cassia, does the fainting soul recruit,
And o'er the fields its fragrant suckers shoot,
                    Like weeds, to harrow.
So grow the plants by thousands o'er the land,
Along the mountain top and water strand,
It is too strange for us to understand,
                    And to our sorrow.

---

glittering ore turned out to be nothing but pyrites, as many a more
modern enthusiast has found out also.

Voor Bye, en Wesp, 't welruykende gebloemt
Is overal: in kleur, en geur geroemd:
Veel meer, als nu mijn *Heldin* heeft genoemd,
        Komt hier te voren.

Daar noyt de hand des Menschen is geweest,
Om iet te doen, tot hulpe siet: dit leest
Men (sonder moeyte en sorg) van 't Veld: en vreest
        Geen werk verloren.

Maar wat de *Konst* (hier boven) noch bedenkt:
En an u schoot (uyt and're Landen) schenkt,
Tot queeking: 't Geen nochtans u niet en krenkt,
        Maar sterkt, in 't voeden.

Is 't smaaklyk Ooft, is alderhande Fruyt;
Is Moes, Sala', Radijs, en lieflijk Kruid
Is Raap, en Kool, die gy op 't beste sluyt,
        En kunt behoeden.

Is bijtend-kruyd, de trekkende Tabak
Is Wortelen: is Malsse-pinstenak:
Meloen, Pompoen, Spansch-spek: dat (met gemak)
        Sich laat genieten.

't Wast alles (wat in andre Landen wast)
Op uwen rug: Ook daar men niet op past:
En sonder veel bekommering en last
        Komt uyt te schieten.

Is Tarw, en Rog', en Garst, en Ert, en Boon,
Is Speld, Majijs, en Boek-weyt, die daar schoon,
En heerlijk wast. Is Haver die den loon
        Wood voor de Paarden.

Is Koe, en Paard, en Schaap, en 't morsig-Swijn,

For bee and wasp, sweet-smelling flowers bloom,
O'er all; renowned for colors and perfume;
More, than my Heroine can yet assume
     To name, occurring.
Wherever men a helping hand accord
To nature, there, behold! the fields reward
Them, without any care; no fears unt'ward
     Of loss them worry'ng.
Whatever skillful science more may know,
And in your lap, from other countries, throw
For culture: these, fresh strength on you bestow,
     Without consuming.
You've most delicious hand and kitchen fruits,
Greens, salads, radishes and savory shoots,
And turnips; and the cabbage you produce,
     In large heads poming.
The biting herb — the strong tobacco plant;
The carrot and the Maltese parsnip; and
The melon, pumpkin, Spanish comfrey, grant
     The sweetest pleasure.
Exotics which, from foreign climes, they bear
Unto your bosom, need no special care;
But reach, untended, in your genial air,
     Their proper measure.
There's wheat and rye; and barley, pea, and bean;
Spelt, maize and buckwheat; all these kinds of grain
Do nobly grow: for horses to sustain,
     Oats are awarded.
You've horses, cows, and wallowing swine and sheep;

Is Gans, en End, en 't Hoen, en 't tam Konijn:
Het wilder al, en vet, en weeld'rig zijn:
                    En veylig aarden.
Het word van *Lucht* en *Aard*, en Vocht vernoegd.
Op 't suyverste, en eelste, t'saam gevoegd:
En werkelijk (als het den akker ploegd)
                    Om voort te teelen.
't Schynt dat NATUUR haar konst, en proefstuk heeft
In u gehad: Om alles watter leefd,
Of wat oyt Land, of volle-Zee uyt-geeft,
                    U meê te deelen.
En dat, op so een wel-gelegen streek
Daar Zee, Revier, en Kil, en Kriek, en Beek
Tot's Menschen dienst, bequaamheyt heeft. Ik spreek
                    Wie heeft daar tegen?
Tot handel, en tot Schip-vaart, uytgesocht:
Met Havens, die den aart zelf heeft gewrocht
Tot heul, van wie in 't lijden word gebrocht:
                    En raakt verlegen.
Dit is het LAND, daar Melk en Honig vloeyd:
Dit is 't geweest, daar 't Kruyd (als dist'len) groeyd:
Dit is de Plaats, daar *Arons-Roode* bloeyd:
                    Dit is het EDEN.
Gelukkig *Land,* gy tergd, en trotst de nijd.
Gy rijst, en klimt, wie dat hat queld, en spijt.
Gy over-wind, wie u geluk bestrijd,
                    God geef u vreede.
God geef u heyl, en voorspoed, troost, en rust.
God bann' de twist, en tweedracht van u Kust.

Geese, ducks and hens; and rabbits (tame to keep)
Which will be all, both fat and choice to eat,
                  And thrive unguarded.

Air, water, soil, of greatest purity;
And all, combined in sweetest harmony,
Unite, the ploughed up land to fructify,
                  With strength unerring.

You seem the masterpiece of nature's hand;
Whatever does with breath of life expand,
Or comes from out the sea, or thrives on land,
                  On you conferring.

And, in a country, fitted happily,
With creek and channel, river, brook and sea,
For every use of man. I make the plea,
                  Who can deny it?

A land for trade and navigation sought;
With harbors which the earth herself has wrought,
For aid to those who are in danger brought
                  And seek to fly it.

It is the land where milk and honey flow;
Where plants distilling perfume grow;
Where Aaron's rod with budding blossoms blow;
                  A very Eden.

Oh happy land! while envy you invite,
You soar far over all you thus excite;
And conquer whom by chance you meet in fight;
                  May God protect and

Defend and save you; peace and comfort give;
All strife and discord from your borders drive;

Dat Nederland u welvaard mach (met lust
　　　　　　　En vreugd) aanschouwen.
Dat yder een (in u) sijn handen werk
Met rust geniet. Dat Christi *Ware-Kerk*
In u (gelijk een Lely) bloey: En 't merk
　　　　　　　Daar van mach houwen.
De Tuchting, en Bond-teekens, en de Leer,
Na 't Suyver-woord, van aller Heeren Heer.
Gerechtigheyt, en Waarheyt: meer en meer:
　　　　　　　Als vaste zuylen.
Waar door en Huys, en Stad, en Land bestaat.
Dat andersins wel licht te gronde gaat.
Als pracht, geweld, on-kuysheyt, nijt en haat
　　　　　　　Daar binnen schuylen.
Maar gy, ô wel, en alder-heerlijkst LAND:
Weest dankbaar, an des milden Gevers hand.
Die u, (als) in een Lust-hof heeft geplant:
　　　　　　　Die gy u kind'ren
Meugt laten, tot een Eeuwig-eygendom
Tot dat het zaad der vrouwen, wederom
Verschijn: tot ons' verlossing: wellekom.
　　　　　　　Wie sal 't hem hind'ren?

　　　　　　　　　　Noch vaster.

So Netherland your happiness perceive
                With joy and pleasure.
So labor may in peace its fruits consume;
And Christ's true Church fresh as the lily bloom,—
Its mark in you irrevocably hewn,
                Henceforth forever.
Rule, doctrine; covenants, all in accord
With His pure word who is, of Lords, the Lord;
Where righteousness and truth may rest like broad
                And solid pillars.
So may a city, house, or kingdom stand,
Which else have laid foundations in the sand,
And envy, pride, hate, lust, and violent hand,
                Lurk in their cellars.
But you accept, O noblest land of all!
With thankfulness, His bounties liberal,
Who has a pleasure garden made your soil,
                That you might render
Your children an inheritance fore'er,
Until the Seed of Woman reappear,
For our redemption. Welcome hour! Who'll dare
                His coming t'hinder?

                      Noch vaster.

PRICKEL-VAERSEN.

Aen de liefhebbers van de volck-planting en broederschap, op te rechte
by de Zuyd-revier van Nieuw-Nederland, door Pieter Cornelis
Plockhoy van Zierick-zee, met sijn medestanders: en de gunstig
voor-rechten (tot dien eynde) van de e. e. achtbare heeren burge
meesteren der stad Amstelredam, haer verleend den 9 van some
maend, 1662.

Ghy arme, die niet wel kond aen u noodruft raken :
Gy rijke, die 't geluck in 't voor-hoofd soecken wild :
Verkiest *Nieuw-neder-land*, ('t sal niemand billik laken)
Eer gy u tijd en macht, hier vruchteloos verspild.
Hier moet gy and'ren, om u dienstb'ren arbeyd troonen,
Daer komt een gulle grond, u werck met woecker loonen.

Nieuw-Neder-land is 't puyck, en 't eelste van de Lande
Een Seegen-rijck gewest, daer Melck en Honigh vloeyd
Dat d'alderhooghste heeft (met dubbeld milde handen)
Begaeft : ja op-gevult, in 't geen daer wast en groeyd.
De Lugt, de Aerd en Zee, sijn swanger met haer gaven
Om (die behoeftigh is) oock sonder moeyt te laven.

't Gevoogelt doofd de lucht, wanneer se sich vervoere
Het wild-gedierte kneust, en plet de vaste grond,

SPURRING-VERSES.

—————— ◂◂●▸▸ ——————

To the lovers of the colony and brothership, to be established on the
South river of New Netherland, by Peter Cornelison Plockhoy of
Zierikzee, with his associates; and the favorable privileges, for
that purpose, granted by the noble Lords Burgomasters of the
city of Amsterdam, the 9th of June, 1662.

You poor, who know not how your living to obtain;
You affluent, who seek in mind to be content;
Choose you New Netherland (which no one shall disdain),
Before your time and strength here fruitlessly are spent.
There have you other ends, your labor to incite;
Your work, will gen'rous soils, with usury, requite.

New Netherland's the flow'r, the noblest of all lands;
With richest blessings crowned, where milk and honey flow;
By the most High of All, with doubly lib'ral hands
Endowed; yea, filled up full, with what may thrive and grow.
The air, the earth, the sea, each pregnant with its gift,
The needy, without trouble, from distress to lift.

The birds obscure the sky, so numerous in their flight;
The animals roam wild, and flatten down the ground;

De Visschen, krielen in de wat'ren: en beroeren
Diens klaerheyd; d'oesters (die men nergens beter vond)
Verheffen hoop op hoop, en maken menigh Eyland:
't Gewas vercierd het bosch: en bou, en hoy, en Wey-land.

Hier hebt ghy deel aen, schoon 't u geld noch moeyte koste.
Maer so gy naerstigh blijft in d'arbeyd op sijn tijd,
(In hoop tot hem, die u uyt d'armoed hier verloste:)
Gy sult een rijken loon: genieten voor u vlijt.
Aen Vee, aen Graen, aen Fruyt: en duysent and're dingen,
Waer door gy stof hebt steeds, d'al-gever lof te singen.

Wat siet gy op u huys, de Stad of 't Land uw's vaders?
Is God niet over-al? den Hemel even wijt?
Sijn segen deckt de aerd: en stort (uyt volle aders)
Een vloed van schatten; die gy vind waer dat gy sijt.
Sy is aen Koning-rijck, noch Vorsten-dom gebonden,
Sy word so wel in 't een, als 't ander Land gevonden.

Maer daer, daer siet gy steeds, een levende vertooningh
Van Eden: en van 't Land, aen Jacobs saad beloofd:
Wie sou in dat gewest (in sulck een 't samen-woningh)
Niet wenschen vry te sijn; en yder hoofd voor hoofd,
Het voor-recht (elck gegund, van d'Amstels-Burger-Heeren)
Genieten? en 't gesach van haer beleydingh eeren?

De 't samen-wooningh is, een grond van alle Staten.
Die eerst gehucht en buert, en Dorp ja Steden maeckt:

The fish swarm in the waters, and exclude the light;
The oysters there, than which none better can be found,
Are piled up, heap on heap, till islands they attain;
And vegetation clothes the forest, mead and plain.

You have a portion there which costs not pains nor gold;
But if you labor give, then shall you also share
(With trust in Him who you from want does there uphold)
A rich reward, in time, for all your toil and care.
In cattle, grain and fruit, and every other thing;
Whereby you always have great cause His praise to sing.

What see you in your houses, towns and Fatherland?
Is God not over all? the heavens ever wide?
His blessings deck the earth,—like bursting veins expand
In floods of treasures o'er, wherever you abide;
Which neither are to monarchies nor duke-doms bound,
They are as well in one, as other country found.

But there, a living view does always meet your eye,
Of Eden, and the promised land of Jacob's seed;
Who would not, then, in such a formed community
Desire to be a freeman; and the rights decreed
To each and every one, by Amstel's burgher lords,
T'enjoy? and treat with honor what their rule awards?

Communities the groundwork are of every state;
They first the hamlet, village and the city make;

Waer uyt 't gemeene-best ontspringt, wiens onder-
saten,
Den welstand van 't geemen (als eygen) 't harte raeckt.
'Tis geen *Vtopia*, 't steund op gegronde wetten :
Die tot de vrijheyd u een vasten Regel setten.

Gy sult geen Vremdelingh, in dese Landen wesen :
Als eertijts ISRAEL, self in ÆGYPTEN was.
Gy hoeft geen dienstbaerheyd, noch dwinglandy te vreesen :
Mits *Iosefs* ogen sien, en letsen op 't Kompas,
De vaders die aen 't Y, haer Stad met lof bestueren.
Sijn u beschermers, en u Land-aerd u gebueren.

Nieuw-neder-lands Zuyd-revier : of 't weede *almasonas*)
Schaft (op haer oevers) u een lusthof : tot verblijf.
Gy kiest of Swanen-dal (daer *Osets*[1] 'rijck en troon was)
Of wel een ander plaats, tot ńut van u bedrijf.
Gy hebt de kuer van al : het staet u vry te kiesen.
Betracht dit voor-recht wel, gy sult het niet verliesen.

Verwerpt dan 't quaed gerucht (on-waerdigh na te luyst'ren)
'Tis uyt wan gunst of haat, of on-kun meest verdicht,

---

[1] Gilles Osset or Hosset was the commander of the colony which was
sent out in 1630-1 to the Hoerekil or Swanendael, on the Delaware, by
Godyn, Van Rensselaer, Bloemart, De Laet and David Pietersz. de Vries
patroons under the West India Company. When de Vries went out, the
next year, be found the colony destroyed ; Osset and the rest of the colonists, thirty-three in number, having been barbarously murdered by the
Indians, and their bodies left to rot in the fields, where they were slain

From whence proceeds the commonwealth; whose mem-
    bers, great
Become, an interest in the common welfare take.
'T is no Utopia; it rests on principles,
Which, for true liberty, prescribes you settled rules.

You will not aliens, in those far lands, appear;
As formerly, in Egypt, e'en was Israel.
Nor have you slavery nor tyranny to fear,
Since Joseph's eyes do see, and on the compass fall.
The civic Fathers who on th' Y perform their labors,
Are your protectors; and your countrymen are neighbors.

New Netherland's South River, — second Amazon,
For you a pleasure garden on its banks concedes.
Choose you the Swanendael, where Osset had his throne,
Or any other spot your avocation needs.
You have the choice of all; and you're left free to choose;
Keep the conditions well, and you have naught to lose.

Discard the base report, unworthy of your ear;
'Tis forged by ignorance and hate and jealous spite,

---

around their half burnt fort. It is this *accident*, as he calls it, the poet
deprecates, in the two following stanzas, from being urged to retard the
proposed attempt to reëstablish a colony in the same region. The city of
Amsterdam had, several years before, sent out other colonists to the South
River who, with some previously settled there under the auspices of the
West India Company, were their countrymen, whom the new colonists
were to find as neighbors.

Van haer die d'oorsaeck sijn : om hatigh te verduyst'ren,
Dees schoone Ochtend-son voor 't lachend middagh-licht.
Aen toe-val mach de saeck wel hind'ren, niet verand'ren,
Maer neemt se wech, gy sult, diens glans en luyster schran-
     d'ren.

'Twas maer een toe-val, die haer stof geeft te verachten,
Dat Land dat (na mijn kun), geen eygen weerga heeft,
Om u (die lust hebt daer te woonen) de gedachten ;
T'ont-roeren buyten 't spoor, eer gy u derwaerts geeft.
Doch sonder re'en en grond, 't geen yder licht kan vatten :
Die tijd en plaats versuymd, verwaerloost groote schatten.

JACOB STEEN-DAM,

Noch vaster.

By those who are its authors, to bedim this fair
Bright morning sun before the laughing noonday light.
An accident may hinder, but not change the plan,
Whose gloss, take that away, you then may fairly scan.

'T was but an accident, which gives them stuff to slight
That land, which, *as I know*, no proper rival has;
In order from your purpose they may you affright,
Who there desire to live, before you thither pass.
'Tis groundless, ev'ry one may easily perceive.
Who now neglects the chance, great treasures does he leave.

JACOB STEENDAM,
                Noch vaster.

MEMOIR AND POEMS

OF

HENRICUS SELYNS.

HENRICUS SELYNS.

There are no written accounts of Henricus Selyns left to us by his contemporaries, and little concerning him has been transmitted by tradition. A few memorials of his ministry of the gospel, to be found in the records of the churches in which he officiated in this country; his letters, while here, to the classis of Amsterdam, his ecclesiastical superiors; occasional minutes in the colonial documents; and casual mention of him by some of the learned men of his time, constitute all the materials, with slight exceptions, now within the reach of his biographer. His life and character can therefore be only imperfectly portrayed, and the interest which the present circumstances have awakened in his name can be only partly satisfied.

It is well known that he was the only clergyman settled in the ministry in Brooklyn before the revolution, and that was during the Dutch rule of the country; and that after the termination of the dynasty of the Hollanders, he was, for many years, the minister of the Dutch Reformed Church in the city of New York; but it has not been so well understood that he was the foremost of the early ministers to enlarge the usefulness of the church to which he belonged, and to secure for it a permanent and independent foundation under the English government of the province. His ministerial duties, indeed, were the great business of his life, occupying principally his time and thoughts, and employing the greatest energies of his nature; and hence it is, that what is extant concerning him relates to him, for the most part, in this character.

As a minister, he possessed in an eminent degree that rare combination of faculties which unites the zeal of the preacher for the salvation of souls, with the prudence of the presbyter for the temporalities of his church. And for this position family tradition, early association, and education united to prepare him. Tracing his ancestry both on the father and mother's side clearly back, through a regular line of elders, deacons and deaconesses, to the first institution of the Dutch Reformed Church as an independent establishment; and connected by blood and marriage with distinguished ministers of that church, he could not fail to imbibe its tenets and principles, and enter with confidence and honorable ambition upon the studies which were to fit him for its service. Hendrick Selyns, his paternal grandfather, was a deacon of the church at Amsterdam, in 1598, and his father an elder from 1639 to 1663; while of the maternal branch, his great grandfather, Hendrick Kock, was a deacon in the same church from 1584 to 1595, and his grandfather, Hans Verklocken, in 1587–90. Agneta Selyns, his grandmother, filled the somewhat peculiar

position, in that church, of deaconess, for several
years. Such is the record,—handed down to us by
himself, of his direct ancestral pledges to this service;
and in the persons of Dominies Triglandius, Lants-
man and Joannes Nieuwenhuysen, distinguished ministers of the church of Amsterdam, who were his
cousins, he felt the influences of collateral relationship to the same end.

He was the son of Jan Selyns and Agneta Kock,
and was born in the city of Amsterdam in the year
1636. Of the incidents of his early life and education we know nothing; except that he was regularly
educated for the ministry, and became proficient in
the various studies required in that office. The
Reformed Church of the Netherlands had at that time
just begun fully to develop its own power and
strength. Sprung from the loins of the Catholic
Church, and reformed from Romanism, its first ministers had been priests of that church. There neces-
sarily were in its origin no ministers who had been
educated to its peculiar form of worship and doctrine.
Among its first duties, therefore, was to provide for
future teachers out of its own youth; and now, at the
period of Selyns, its universities and course of study
had fairly come into operation for that purpose. He
in due time became a proponent, — the first step in
the ministry, a kind of candidate for full orders. In
the earliest period of this Reformed Church its teachers, in consequence of the want of ministers growing

out of the circumstances of the separation, fully qualified to fill the office entire, were divided into ministers and prophets; the former exclusively being
authorized to preach and administer the sacraments,
and the latter being charged simply with the office of
explaining a portion of the scriptures to the congregation upon certain days every one or two weeks. The
college of prophets was, however, soon abolished,
and proponents, as they were called, substituted in
their places, — being the young men, now that the
church was established, who had graduated at the
universities with a view to the ministry. They were
examined for this purpose before the theological
faculty, or a classis, and if approved, were then
licensed *proponere*, to make propositions from the
pulpit, or preach, but not to administer the sacraments. This examination was called *preparatory.* A
second one, the *peremptory*, took place whenever the
proponent received a call from a congregation, when,
if it were satisfactory, he was installed with the full
powers of a minister, than which, no other or higher
priestly office exists in this church.[1]

---

[1] *Ypey and Dermout*, I, 384–6. Although the name of proponent
has fallen into disuse, the same system of double examinations
exists in this church in this country at the present day.—*Demarest*,
183. In the time of Selyns these examinations were conducted with
great rigor, lasting sometimes for a month. In some of the provinces of the Netherlands they were conducted in the Latin language.
A thorough knowledge of the scriptures, of doctrinal theology, the
systems of the ancient philosophy and of the dead languages was
necessary on the part of the candidate.

It was while he was officiating as a proponent that Henricus Selyns received a call to become the minister of the church at Breukelen in New Netherland, made, by the Dutch West India Company, through the classis of Amsterdam. Such was the general practice in this colony during the ascendancy of that company, although it has ever been a cardinal principle of the Dutch Reformed Church, affirmed as early as the Synod of Antwerp, that the servants of God, the ministers, elders and deacons, are only properly chosen when they are designated by a lawful election of the congregation. It was at that time an exceptional practice in New Netherland for the congregation to make their applicatiou for a minister to the West India Company, because the company generally paid or contributed to his salary. In the case of Selyns one half was to be paid by the company and one half by the congregation, which was also to furnish a house for his residence.

At that time the congregation at Breukelen was both small and poor. It numbered twenty-seven persons, men and women, in all, and they were scattered among four hamlets, in different parts of the territory of the present city of Brooklyn, known then and still by the distinct names of Cujanes, the Waaleboght, Breukelen, and the Ferry. The population of the whole town was one hundred and ninety-four souls. This church had been under the pastoral charge of the Rev. Johannes Theodorus Polhemus,

who resided at Midwout, now called Flatbush, and
who ministered to the church there and at Amersfoort, now known as Flatlands. But he was getting
old, and the road between Midwout and Breukelen,
where he came to perform religious services alter-
nately on Sundays, with the two other towns, being
rocky and hilly, it was difficult and dangerous for him
to travel. Such were the reasons assigned for the call
of a minister for Breukelen alone. Selyns accepted
the call; he was peremptorily examined by the classis
of Amsterdam, and, on the 16th of February, 1660,
was admitted to the ministry with full powers. He
engaged, however, to serve the congregation at
Breukelen for the term of four years only. He sailed
a few weeks afterwards in one of the company's ships,
in company with the Rev. Harmanus Blom, who had
been examined at the same time with him, for the
purpose of supplying the church at Esopus, afterwards
called Kingston. They arrived at New Amsterdam
in July of that year. Governor Stuyvesant, who, by
virtue of his position as Director General of the
colony, accredited all public functionaries, ecclesiastical as well as civil, in the colony, was then absent at
Esopus negotiating a peace with the Indians: and
when the treaty was concluded, his absence was still
further prolonged by a visit to Fort Orange. To both
these settlements the two young ministers followed
him, in order to deliver their letters, so that it was
not until the 7th of September that Mr. Selyns was
formally inducted into his church.

This ceremony, measured by the usual standard of great events, was, indeed, insignificant; but viewed as the first installation of a minister in what is now a large and flourishing city, the third in size in the United States, and as populous as the famous city of Amsterdam herself at the present day, it was one which deserved, as it received, the attention of the authorities in an appropriate and becoming manner. It was, nevertheless, to that colony an interesting event, and it was accompanied by proceedings calculated to give dignity and authority to the minister. The governor deputed two of his principal officers to present the minister to the congregation. Nicasius de Sillé, a member of the council, a man of no mean literary attainments and well versed in the law, and Martin Krigier, burgomaster of New Amsterdam, who on several important occasions was the envoy of the governor to the adjoining English colonies. After the presentation, Dom. Selyns preached his inaugural sermon, and then read the call of the classis and their certificate of examination, with a testimonial from the ministers of Amsterdam, declaring that during the time he had dwelt among them, he had not only diligently used the holy ordinances of God for the promotion of his own salvation, but had also often edified their church by his acceptable preaching; and, moreover, had by his life and conversation demeaned himself as a godly and pious man, — a character which he never forfeited. The duties in which he was now installed he continued to discharge for the prescribed term with zeal and fidelity. The records of the church at Breukelen for this period, are still preserved in his own handwriting, and bear ample evidence of his devotion to his calling, chronicling, with rare simplicity, the occurrences in the government of the church and the occasions of discipline of his flock. Once we find him in collision with the magistrates of the town in regard to an attempted jurisdiction ´ on their part over an act of ecclesiastical censure exercised by him towards one of the church members. In a respectful letter he refused to appear before them or acknowledge their right to take cognizance of the sentence pronounced by him and his consistory. He maintained that the civil courts could not try offences arising purely out of the ecclesiastical relation; and that the complainant having submitted himself to the canons of the church by becoming one of its members, was thereby precluded from taking the matter before the courts. In this, as in some other trying occasions of his life, when he was brought in conflict with others upon questions of authority and power, he sustained the rights and privileges of his official position with equal firmness, dignity and force of reasoning. His pen and logic were never to be despised by his opponents. In his controversy with the magistrates of Breukelen his arguments prevailed.

During this stage of his ministry he married his first wife, Machtelt Specht, daughter of Herman

tot Vaderlijcke onttreninge en medeedogentheyt. Maer alles
loeft de goede God, die gesprooten zij, gebracht tot lesten met
de lagte besieedende der schepen; de Engelsche tot stilte en
vreeden tot vreede, onse wreedlagen tot lestangde ende Matiede
sjcke Sasdagen tot den dag van danckseggings, des verleeden
Woonsdag tot belesijt der Voorgdou Bededagen gehouden is, God
zij danck, dit de Oorloogen doot ophouden tot aen het ōijnde
der Abde, den bogoverhoockt en spiske in wode stadt. Ende
Hiermede, Seer Eerwaardige, Gootsaljed in Hooggelecede
Broeder in Christo Jesu, zijt den solode God bevoten tot de
Voemaetinge der Heijligen, ende opbovinge dis lichaem J.
Christi Bald. Actum Breuckelen in N. Nederlt. den 9 Junij 1664

Uwer Eerwaardig.

Onderdanighste Broeder in Christo Jesu,

9 Junne 1664   Henricus Selijns.

good God has brought all to pass for the
best, with his look arrival of the shipping,
the English to grief and the envious to
peace; our lamentations to songs of joy
and our monthly fast days to a day of
thanksgiving, which was observed on last
Thursday, which was set apart for a
day of prayer. God be thanked, who
caused war to cease to the end of the
earth, and breaks the spear in two. And
reverent very reverend, godly and highly
learned brothers in Christ I commend may
God order the same for the perfection
of the saints and the edification of
the body of Christ Church. Love of God
given in New Netherland the 9 of June
1664.

Your Reverend
Humble brother in Christ Jesus
Reverend Polyard.

(Addressed to the
Classis of Amsterdam.)

Specht of the city of Utrecht, a young lady, if we may trust his own description of her, of rare personal beauty and worth. He has transmitted her portrait to us in a birthday ode, commencing,

" Siet de Stichtse nymphjens loopen,"

one of the prettiest pictures that conjugal affection has ever drawn. These lines, apparently, were composed shortly after his return from this country to Holland. The marriage was solemnized at New Amsterdam on the 9th of July, 1662.

In the following year took place the horrible massacre of the Dutch settlers by the Indians at Esopus, the residence of his fellow voyager and colleague in the ministry, Dom. Blom. This tragical occurrence produced a deep impression upon the minds of the colonists, and was made the theme by Dom. Selyns of one of his longest poetical effusions. The marriage of Aegidius Luyck, rector of the Latin School in New Amsterdam, was the occasion of an epithalamium in which he introduces a description of the scene. He alludes to some natural occurrences which he regards as omens presaging the calamity. This allusion is the more noticable, because it is the only reference to be found in the writings of the colonists, to the great earthquake and meteoric phenomena which in 1664 visited the northern parts of this continent, and which, according to reliable authorities, were probably the most terrific and extraordinary convulsions of nature which the earth has experienced within the period of authentic profane history.[1]

Although designated to take charge of the church at Breukelen, Mr. Selyns did not confine his pastoral duties to that town. In order to make out a sufficient salary, Governor Stuyvesant engaged him to preach on Sunday evenings to a congregation of boors and negroes at his bouwery, or farm, in the suburbs of New Amsterdam. These negroes, about forty in number, were the manumitted slaves of the West India Company, to whom a plot of land, designated as the negro quarter, had been assigned for their habitations in that vicinity. But although they themselves were freed, their children were nevertheless held in bondage. The religious condition of this unfortunate class is referred to in one of the letters of Dom. Selyns, and his remark is not without interest. "The negroes," he writes, "have requested us at times to baptize their children, but we have refused to do so, partly on account of their want of knowledge and belief, and partly on account of the material and perverted object which they had in view, and which was nothing else than liberating their children from bodily slavery, without striving after godliness and Christian virtue. We have, nevertheless, as was becoming, used every means to the extent of our ability, for their instruction by public and private

---

[1] Some interesting particulars of this remarkable earthquake will be found in a note to the poem referred to here, on a subsequent page.

catechizing, but with little success among the old, who have no faculty of comprehension. Better promise has been given by the young who have reasonably improved."[1] The old negroes, of whose dullness of intellect he complains, were natives of Africa and had been introduced into the colony by the company. Between this humble and almost barren field of labor, and his Breukelen congregation, Selyns assiduously applied his time and attention for the four years of his engagement. During that time the church at Breukelen increased in numbers four-fold. As the expiration of the term grew near, however, he looked anxiously forward to his return to his native land, to fulfill, as he said, "another obligation which we all owe to those who have begotten us,"—to gladden the eyes of his aged parents. He applied to the authorities both here and in Fatherland for leave to go home, and received it with honorable testimony of having fully and satisfactorily fulfilled his obligations. He left accordingly, in July, 1664, a few days before the colony fell into the hands of the English. When he left he undoubtedly did so with no intention or expectation of returning to America. He had come out here originally as to a preparatory school to fit himself for some more extended sphere of duty at home.

He appears to have remained unsettled for two years after his return to Holland. In 1666 he was in

---

[1] Letter to the classis, 9th June, 1664.

charge of the congregation at Waverveen, near
Utrecht, a rural village whose inhabitants gained their
subsistence principally by bagging turf. He has left
us some sprightly lines commemorative of this place.
Waverveen was not then nor has it since been a place
of any importance; and as yet Selyns was transferred
to no higher position than at Breukelen. Its poverty,
its turf and people he thus epigrammatizes :

> Geen koude liën zyn meer te vrèen,
> Dan met ons Waverveensche veen:
> Schoon't veen wordt asch en veen-liëns armer;
> Maer acht 'et voor geen schaed noch schand,
> Dat 't kindt syn moeder treedt en brandt,
> En macht syn vriendt en broeder warmer.

> Though burns the turf,— the people poor,
> Upon our Waverveen's peat moor,
> None to be viewed with more alarm are ;
> But let it not arouse your ire,
> The child its mother sets on fire,
> To make its friend and brother warmer.

In 1675 we find he was appointed chaplain in the
army of the states for that year ;[1] but with the circumstances of his connection with the army we are
unacquainted. It took place, however, at a critical
period of the history of the Netherlands, — when
France and England conspired together, and found
allies in the German princes to assist them, in the
humiliation of the provinces. Whether this was the
first introduction of Selyns into the army or whether
he was again appointed does not appear, but it is evi-
dent he was no unconcerned witness of the efforts to

---

[1] Veeris. Kerk. Al. Noord Holl. 137.

destroy his native country. One of these German princes was the war prelate, the Bishop of Munster, who invaded Groningen and Overyssel. The only verses of Selyns known to be in print, in Holland, are to be found upon a plate representing the breaking of the dyke which this bishop constructed, eight miles long, in the summer of 1763 for the purpose of contracting the river Vecht, in front of the city of Coevenden, so as to cause the waters to rise and submerge the city and drown out the inhabitants if they would not surrender. The dyke was in fact finished, the waters were rising and had already risen above the counterscarps of the fortifications of the town, the bishop was boasting of a certain victory, when deliverance came to the citizens from a higher power than man. A violent storm agitating the body of waters caused them to break through the dyke in several places at the same time, drowning five hundred of the besiegers and compelling the bishop to raise the siege and retire.[1] It is this event that the lines of Selyns commemorate.

> Hoe wroet de Bischop met syn myter is het slyck
> En stuwt het water op, om Coevenden te winnen!
>   Hy breeckt syn hoge eedt, Godt breeckt syn hoge dyck,
> Die sonder Godt begint, wat baet 'et te beginnen?
>   By Groningen was 't vyer, nu 't water sonder vrucht.
> Strydt, Bischop, strydt niet meer, oft strydt met aard en lucht.

> His mitre in the mire, how did the Bishop strike,
> And dam the water up, so Coeverden to win!
>   He breaks his lofty oath, God breaks his lofty dyke.
> Who without God begins, what boots it to begin?

---

[1] Holl. Merc. Oct. 1673, p. 201–2.

At Groningen 'twas the *fire ;* now, of fruit the *water's* bare.
Strive, Bishop, strive no more, or strive with *earth* and *air.*

With the exception of his temporary chaplaincy in
the army, Selyns passed sixteen years of his life in
the obscurity of Waverveen without any noticeable
incident which has come down to us in his career.
We do, indeed, find him presiding, during this time,
over an ecclesiastical meeting called at Waverveen for
ordination of a minister, but that is all. He seems to
have been content with his position, than which none
can be imagined less desirable, in preference to
the highest place in the American church ; for in
1670, upon the death of Rev. Joannes Megapolensis
of New York, he received and declined a call from
the church there to become associated with the Rev.
Samuel Drisius in its charge. But at a later period
he changed his mind. Upon the death of Drisius
and of the Rev. William Nieuwenhuysen, who had
taken the place which had been declined by Selyns, the
call was urgently renewed by the same church ; and
he then accepted.[1] He accordingly left his native
land again, and now for the last time, to cast his lot
for life in America. He arrived at New York in the
summer of 1682, where he was received "by the
whole congregation with great affection and joy."
The recollections of his former ministrations were
fresh in their minds, and both pastor and people were
happy in an already tried relationship with each other.

---

[1] De Witt's Dis. on Coll. Dutch Church, 70.

But he had now entered upon a more extended and arduous field of labor than he had ever filled before, and he devoted himself to it with zeal and industry. His own account, immediately after his arrival at New York, will best explain his work. " On my arrival here I commenced preaching three times a week, and have carried out my purpose thus far; but as the number of the people attending the church both from the city and its suburbs is greater than the church can accommodate, it is in contemplation to build a new one, or, at least, to make more room by means of a large gallery. I devote Sunday evenings to catechizing the children, who multiply in this country more than in any other part of the world. In addition to this, I have agreed to preach at Bergen, a place situated on the river, three Mondays in the year, morning and evening, and to administer the Lord's supper. I found a new church there and administered the communion to 134 members. At other times they attend service here. The Harlem people come here to the Lord's supper, but I have promised to preach there once a year for the purpose of confirming elders and deacons. They have nominated to us, conformably to a certain understanding of the 19th of June, 1672, a double number of elders and deacons, out of which a single member is to be chosen for the consistory, which will now be confirmed. With this exception, there is no difference as regards church government, between you and the

Netherlanders in all this country. We hold Divine service both here and in the rural districts, wherever it is important, publicly, in delightful quiet and without the least difficulty.

"We and the English inhabitants use the same church. They perform their services at the conclusion of ours, by reading the Common Prayer. They have a clerk, but no minister, except one who marries and baptizes in private houses, but does not preach. There is here a Lutheran church and minister, who lives in this city in summer and at Albany in winter. Besides these, there are Quakers, Jews and Labadists; the Quakers being most numerous, the Jews next, and the Labadists the least. The last are in the habit of attending my rest-day preaching, both morning and evening, but afternoons assemble by themselves. As regards papists there are none, or else they come with us or the Lutherans." [1]

In order to understand this allusion to the Labadists, it may be necessary to recall a forgotten chapter in our early history. In the latter part of 1679, two speaking brothers, as they were called, of the followers of John de Labadie, came from Wiewaard in Friesland to New York on a tour of exploration for a place to found a colony of that sect. After traveling over Long Island and Staten Island, up the North River to Albany, and eastward to Boston, and traversing New Jersey, and along the Delaware, they finally

---

[1] Letter to the classis of Amsterdam, October 28th, 1682.

determined upon a site in Maryland, where they actually formed a settlement on the manor of Augustine Heermans, called New Bohemia. In order to aid this settlement they sought proselytes in New Amsterdam. The Labadists professed the doctrines of the Dutch church, but adopted some peculiarities more of practice than faith, not very dissimilar to those of the Shaking Quakers of modern times. These two brethren spent much of their time in New York, from whence they made their journeys of observation of the country, and where, in fact, they obtained the members of their new community. A son of Augustine Heermans, residing in New York, was one of their principal converts, and through him they obtained the lands in Cecil county in Maryland, where they finally settled.

Dom. Selyns gives some further explanations of the proceedings of the two tourists in a letter to Rev. Willem a-Brakel, who wrote a volume on the doctrines of the Labadists. Speaking of them, Mr. Selyns, writing from New York, to that distinguished divine, says: "In order not to be taken for Labadists,— though neither the name nor doctrine were known in these parts,— they came over here under assumed names. P. Schluyter took the name of Vorsman, and Jas. Dankers, that of Schilder. This being exposed, they said it was done in order that they might not be written after, and, especially, that these were their apostolic names. They regularly attended church and said they had nothing against my doctrines; that they were of the Reformed church, and stood by the Heidelberg Catechism and Dordrecht confession. Vorsman gave himself out as a physician, but *unsuccessful in practice*, and Schilder as a wine-racker. Afterwards, in order to lay the ground-work for a schism, they began holding meetings with closed doors, and to rail out against the church and consistory, as Sodom and Egypt, and saying they must separate from the church; they could not come to the service, or hold communion with us. They then absented themselves from the church. And I may say they were more employed in obtaining persons of different trades than of godliness, who will find when it is too late that they have been cheated; for they are required to sell their houses and goods, leave this land of darkness, and go to New Bohemia, which is the true land of Goshen. I fear it will terminate fatally."[1]

The prophecy of Dom. Selyns in relation to the fate of those persons who were seduced into the attempt to form the settlement at New Bohemia was fulfilled. The colony dwindled away, and the land, early in the last century, passed into other hands. Like the parental society at Wiewaard, it is now merely a memorial for the historian to illustrate the folly of men and women proposing to live together in cloister life, with a community of property and goods.

---

[1] Leere en Leydinge der Labadisten, Ed. Rott. 1738, p. 56–7.

The colony in Maryland scandalized the brethren in Fatherland by becoming slaveholders, and relapsing into other practices of the inhabitants of the country, inconsistent with the views of the founder of the sect. The true nature of man both here and there asserted its power, and the entire social theories and doctrines of De Labadie dissolved before the fire of human passion enkindled in the human bosom by the Creator for wise and certain purposes. [1]

---

[1] The colony of the Labadists was planted on a piece of the territory granted to Augustine Heermans, a Bohemian, and an inhabitant of New Amsterdam, by the first Lord Baltimore, for his services in preparing a map of Maryland. This patent was at the junction of what is now called Bohemia river and the Elk river, where they empty into the Chesapeake, and was called Bohemia Manor. The land of the colony borders on the line of the state of Delaware, but lies, with the exception of a few acres in the state of Maryland. Ephraim Heermans, a son of Augustine, was, at the time of the visit of the two Labadists to New York, employed in one of the public offices, and became a convert to their system, from which he, however, afterwards apostatized. Through his instrumentality, as observed in the text, his father conveyed, in 1683, to Peter Sluyter, or Vorsman and others, land to the amount of 3750 acres, upon which the colony was actually established. The whole of the land thus conveyed, soon afterwards passed into the sole proprietorship of Sluyter or Vorsman. In 1698 a partition was made and Sluyter conveyed to the members of the colony portions in severalty. In 1722 he made his will, by which he devised his own portion to his son-in-law, Petrus Bouchell. Peter Bayard, of New York, was one of the original grantees, and was probably one of the members of his congregation, alluded to by Dom. Selyns, led off by the new doctrine. He, however, withdrew from the colony, and on the partition Sluyter conveyed his portion to his son, Samuel Bayard, whose descendants continued in possession of it until 1789. The land upon which the manor-house of Bohemia manor stood belongs at the present time, or did recently belong, to Hon. Richard H. Bayard of Delaware.

We are indebted for the facts in relation to the title of the lands of

Selyns now occupied an important position in the churches of the province. His congregation was not only the largest in the country, but it embraced among its members men of the highest social and political standing, who for many years exerted great influence in the government, among whom may be particularly mentioned Stephanus Van Cortlandt, Nicholas Bayard, Joannes De Peyster and Dr. Johannes Kerfbyl. His church was at the seat of government,—the metropolis, where the other churches of the colony naturally looked for aid and advice. Moreover, he had assumed its duties at a most critical period in the history of the ecclesiastical affairs of the Dutch inhabitants, when the greatest wisdom and prudence were requisite to preserve their religious privileges. The political character, and with it the ecclesiastical relations of the country, had entirely changed during his absence in Holland. The English conquest had taken place, and the colonies had, by treaty stipulations, been irretrievably transferred to British rule. General ecclesiastical jurisdiction over the land no longer centered in the classis of Amster-

---

the Labadists on Bohemia manor to George L. Davis, Esq., of Baltimore, the author of *The Day Star of American Freedom*, who kindly communicated to us the documents from which they are derived. The reader may also consult Mr. Davis's interesting volume for further information. For the earlier history of the colony at New Bohemia the only printed source of information is Dittelbach's *Verval en Val der Labadisten*, Amst. 1692. Some later particulars may be gathered from the journal of Samuel Bownas, the Quaker preacher, who visited the colony in 1702, and found there a community of about one hundred persons.

dam; and its special authority over the Dutch churches here, was entirely without legal sanction. In contemplation of law, the members of these churches were in the position of separatists or dissenters from the established church of England, and were tolerated only under the articles of the surrender, which provided that the Dutch should " enjoy liberty of their consciences in divine worship and church discipline." When Selyns arrived in New York, the country was under the proprietary government of the Duke of York. No provision of law had been made to secure these privileges. Governor Andros had actually inducted, by authority of the Duke of York, the Rev. Nicholas Renslaer, an Episcopalian clergyman, as minister of the Dutch church at Albany, — an act of prerogative which Domine Nieuwenhuysen and the consistories of New York and Albany, resisted with the greatest determination.[1] This action on the part of the Duke's government shows, on the one hand, how that government understood its powers, and on the other how highly the inhabitants prized the right of choosing their own ministers. The Duke exercised absolute and arbitrary power through governors of his own appointment.

---

[1] Upon this question, all the Dutch churches of the colony made common cause and resisted the induction of Dom. Renslaer, as a dangerous precedent. Nieuwenhuysen, was the minister of the church at New York, and the immediate predecessor of Selyns. Jacob Leísler, who afterwards became the people's governor of the province, also violently opposed the act, and was imprisoned in consequence. See *Col. Hist.* III, 526.

Governor Nicoll proclaimed at Hempstead, immediately after the conquest, in 1664, a code of laws for the government of the Duke's territories, collected out of the laws in force in the other British colonies; but that made no provision for allowing the churches the privileges which they had formerly enjoyed. It gave toleration of opinion but expressly authorized the majority of the inhabitants of any town to call, and maintain by tax on the town, *any* protestant minister. The Dutch population were, therefore, uneasy and dissatisfied. The right of calling a minister should be in the congregation, and they alone should be liable for his support. They, therefore, hailed the announcement with joy, when, on the arrival of Governor Dongan, in 1683, it was proclaimed that an assembly of the people was to be immediately convoked, with power to enact proper laws. To the establishment of the rights and privileges of the Dutch churches, on this occasion, Selyns was fully alive.

Although the political and legal relations between the American churches and the church in Holland had been effectually and finally severed, the ecclesiastical authority of the latter continued to be exercised and acknowledged among the Dutch themselves, the same as before the conquest. Ministers were still appointed by the classis of Amsterdam, and to that body they rendered an account of their stewardship. Ordination for the holy office was, indeed, sometimes made here,[1] but the recipient was subjected to the same classical jurisdiction and accountability. This relation was observed as a matter both of necessity and inclination on the part of the poeple. There were no adequate means in this country, at first, otherwise to supply the pulpits with proper preachers; and on the other hand, the hearts of the Dutch yearned towards the institutions of the land of their ancestors. This dependence of the colonists upon Holland for spiritual teachers, begat the exercise of authority by those there who supplied their wants. A correspondence, more or less close, was kept up by letter between the ministers and the classis. Dom. Selyns wrote regularly once a year, and sometimes oftener, explaining the condition of his church. His letters frequently threw light on the movements of other churches than those of the Dutch, and on public affairs generally, and possess additional historical interest for that reason.

One feature of these communications, forcibly striking the mind of the reader, is the catholic spirit in which he always speaks of other denominations

---

[1] Such, at least, was the earliest practice of the church in this country, although it was different at a later period, when candidates for ordination were compelled to go to Holland for the purpose. Peter Tesschenmacher, the Dutch minister at Schenectady, who was massacred by the French and Indians, when they burned that city, was ordained by an ecclesiastical assembly of the ministers of the Dutch churches in this province at New York, in 1678, for the purpose of taking charge of the church at New Castle, where he remained until 1682, when, in consequence of some disagreement with his congregation, he left, and accepted a call from Schenectady.

and ministers.   In his confidential intercourse with his superiors he might be expected to have exhibited some sectarian spirit in regard to their progress or merits; yet we find nothing of the kind in them, but, on the contrary, expressions of satisfaction at their success; and where he does condemn, it is easy to be seen that he does so on no narrow or selfish grounds. A character so liberal and amiable could not help endearing him to those around him, and inviting their confidence. We find him, accordingly, not only beloved by his own congregation, but on terms of friendship with the heads of the government and his colleagues in the other churches in New York, and in correspondence with distinguished men in the neighboring colonies. He was probably known to the ministers at Boston, at the time of his first residence in New Netherland, as we find among his poems one in Latin upon some verses addressed by the Rev. John Wilson, the first minister of Boston, to Governor Stuyvesant.[1] But his correspondence with them after his return to New York was frequent.

---

[1] Mr. Wilson died in 1667, and, consequently, when Selyns was not in this country. This poem, therefore, must have been written before he left for Holland. His subsequent correspondence with Cotton Mather, not only appears from various intimations in his letters and his laudatory poem prefixed to the Magnalia, but from the direct testimony, furnished by Senguerdius, of Selyns himself.

Mr. Wilson's verses to Governor Stuyvesant are probably lost. We are, therefore, unable to state the occasion of his writing them; but of his habit of thus addressing persons, Cotton Mather remarks, " that he had so nimble a faculty of putting his devout thoughts into verse that he signalized himself by the greatest frequency, perhaps,

He speaks in no less kindly terms of William Penn, who arrived in this country about this time, while he expresses his condemnation of the enthusiastic principles, as he styles them, of the Quakers. Many of the Dutch families remained on the Delaware after the arrival of Penn, and became denizens of his proprietorship. Selyns warned them against his religious doctrines. In his letters he briefly touches upon these different topics of interest to the church. Thus he wrote to the classis: "I received no answer from you by Domine Dellius,[1] It is impossible for me to neglect this correspondence. I may forget my right hand, but you never. * * * I have commenced a regular catechizing of an hundred youth in the summary of the Heidelbergh catechism.

---

that ever man used, of sending poems *to all persons, in all places, on all occasions;* and upon this, as well as upon greater accounts, was a David unto the flocks of our Lord in the wilderness." *Magnalia,* III, 41.

[1] Rev. Godfridus Dellius, minister at Albany, arrived here from Holland in August, 1683. He was a man of learning, and devoted much attention to the conversion of the Mohawk Indians living in and around Albany; but he became obnoxious to the colonial government, and was finally compelled to leave his church and return to Europe, in 1699. He obtained from Governor Fletcher a grant of land on the North river, above Saratoga, seventy miles long by twelve wide, and another on the Mohawk, in conjunction with William Pinhorn and Evert Bancker, fifty miles in length. Both grants were afterwards vacated by act of assembly, for extravagance and want of consideration. Lord Bellamont gave a terribly severe account of him to the lords of trade, (IV *Col. Hist.* 488–90), but that governor was so much prejudiced against the Anti-Leislerian party that his statements should be received with great caution. Dellius applied, through his agent here, to the assembly, in 1714, for some arrears due him, and obtained the payment of one half the amount.

This is gone through with every three months, and from them are admitted to the church those who are fit, after a public confession. This is to my church a great benefit, to my consistory, a satisfaction, and to my own soul, a comfort. * * * *

"I have nothing to complain of on the score of entertainment. My congregation is engaged in building for me a large house, three stories high, all of stone, and based on a foundation of unmerited love. The neighboring villages,— though too much for one person to attend to, — I have not suffered to be neglected, preaching there Mondays and Thursdays, or administering the Lord's supper, thanks-preaching, and performing church confirmation. I am sustained by the power of God. How much more is it manifest in my infirmity!

" Domine Peter Daillè, late professor at Salmurs, has become my colleague. He is full of fire, godliness and learning. Banished on account of his religion, he maintains the cause of Jesus Christ with untiring zeal. Rev. John Gordon has come over for the purpose of taking charge of the service in the English Church. * * *

"Lord Dongan, our new governor, has arrived at last, and has informed me and my consistory that his orders from the Duke were to allow liberty of conscience. His excellency is a man of information, politeness and affability. I have had the pleasure to receive a call from him, and am permitted to call upon him whenever I desire. The next assembly, which is convoked for the purpose of enacting reasonable laws for us and our posterity, will determine what is best for the country and church.

"At New Castle, where Domine Coelman was called, it is quiet.[1] On Sundays a sermon is read, but the people are too few in number to support a minister. Some of them, particularly those of means, have left. By reason of William Penn's coming over, and government, a great change has taken place there. His Honor, who is a very eloquent man, preaches himself, and preaches learnedly. I would not advise any one, with the uncertainty as regards these enthusiasts, to go there as a minister.

"The position of the church in New England is better. At Harvard, there is a college which sends forth much learning, and many learned men, as appears by the accompanying list.[2] Domine Caleb, an Indian, is a minister among the Indians. At

---

[1] This relates to Rev. Jacobus Coelman of Sluys, in Flanders, who had embraced Labadism, and for that reason was called by the church at New Castle on the Delaware, where Sluyter and Danckers had secured a controlling influence. Coelman, however, did not come. He probably had already, before the action of the congregation at New Castle, renounced Labadism, as he published, in 1683, an exposure of its errors in a work under the title of *Historisch Verhael nopende der Labadisten, scheuringh en veelerley dwalingen met de weder leggingh der selver*. He likens the dancing of the Labadists to that of the *Derrises* and of the Indians in New Netherland, in their *Kintekaye*, or *Cantica*, of which he seems to speak of his personal knowledge as if he had once been in this country, p. 105.

[2] The list inclosed was a catalogue of Harvard College, to which it has been presented, it being the only copy in existence of that date.

Boston, the capital of New England, there are four ministers.[1] I have been welcomed by them by letter, and have, *exceptis excipiendis* κοινονιῶν δεξιῶς from the same. They assimilate to the Presbyterians, especially as regards baptism.

"From the letters of Dom. Voshuyl and a passenger from Curaçao, we learn that the condition of the church there is good, but, in consequence of the failure of commerce, many are inclined to come and settle here. There have been no ships this year from Surinam."[2]

The hopes entertained in regard to the action of the assembly were hardly realized. It was the first assembly of the people ever held in the province. Heretofore the laws, like the code promulgated at Hempstead, came ostensibly from the court of assizes, composed of the justices of the peace. The new assembly met on the 17th of October, 1683. On the 30th of the same month, it passed an act "for the better establishing the government of the province, and that justice and right might be done equally to all persons within the same." Besides affirming the civil rights of the people, it declared what were their religious privileges and established the legal position,

---

[1] These were Rev. James Allen, of the First Church, Rev. Increase Mather of the North Church, and Rev. Samuel Willard of the Old South, all men of eminence in their day. The fourth was, probably, the no less eminent Rev. Cotton Mather, who was then officiating as an assistant to his father in the North Church, though he was not ordained as its pastor until the next year.

[2] Letter to the classis, October, $\frac{21}{31}$, 1683.

of the churches. It provided that all the existing
Christian churches of the province should " be held
and reputed as privileged churches, and enjoy all
their former freedom of their religion in Divine
worship and church discipline, and that all former
contracts made and agreed on for the maintenance of
the several ministers of the said churches shall stand
and continue in full force and virtue, and that all contracts for the future to be made, should be of the
same power." This was a full recognition of the
right of the churches to contract for their own ministers. The statute is known as the Duke's *charter of
liberties and privileges*, and as such is found still in our
modern collections of the statutes. But, in truth, it
never became an operative law. If it ever received
the sanction of the Duke, it, on the contrary, was
rejected by him as king, in council, on the 3d of
March, 1685, — this province having been devolved on
the crown by the accession of the Duke to the throne,
on the death of Charles. One of the objections presented against the act by the council was, that the
provision for confirming the contracts of the several
ministers, although agreeable to the practice in New
England, was not conformable to that of the other
plantations. The statute, invalid as it was, is important,
however, because it shows the relative feelings of the
people, and the crown, and the commencement of the
struggle here for religious freedom. It indicates,
moreover, the direction of the efforts of the Dutch

churches to secure their independence of the crown.[1]

Sir Edward Andros, the former governor of New York, who had been appointed governor of New England, succeeded Dongan as governor again of New York, with New Jersey, in 1688, thus including all the provinces north and east of Pennsylvania under his jurisdiction. So New York ceased to be governed as a separate province. But this change in the form of government brought no change in the policy towards the churches. They continued by sufferance merely to enjoy those rights which were contemplated in the charter of liberties and privileges. Dom. Selyns devoted himself in the meanwhile assiduously to the duties of his calling, communicating regularly as usual by letter to the classis.

" Sir Edward Andros," he writes, Oct. 10, 1688, " Governor at Boston, who has now also entered upon the government of New York and Jersey, having thus in charge the country from Canada to Pennsylvania, belongs to the church of England. Understanding and speaking both Low Dutch and French he attends my preaching and that of M. Daillè. The rising thundergust of schismatic Labadism and the *bruta et brutalia* lightning of fantastic Quakerism have mostly vanished, without more ado, into smoke. Vorsman and his company, comprise, at the highest, twelve Labadistic apostles, and are striving to fill up

---

[1] This statute may be found in the Revised Laws of 1813, Vol. 2. appendix. As to its rejection by both the assembly and the crown, see the resolutionof the assembly, in 1691, and *Col. Hist.* III. 159–357.

their graveyard in New Bohemia. It will finally come to naught. Tellenaer has packed up his Quaker goods in order to become a justice of the peace in a village in Pennsylvania. To subsist without God was an impossible thing. Would that sin could be so diminished and godliness thus increased through the whole land. But dykes and dams break through, more and more, and place this land in the most miserable flood of unrighteousness. God preserve us from more sin and keep us from proportionate punishment.

"It has pleased the Lord to visit this city and most of the country with a new kind of measles, and a relapsing of the same. Dom. Schaats of New Albany, arrived at his 80th year, begins to fail and preaches once a fortnight. This patriarch may at any moment be removed to the land of the patriarchs. Our French brethren are doing well, and their congregations increase remarkably by the daily arrival of French fugitives. At New Castle the French minister is dead. About five leagues from here, where Nova Rupella (New Rochelle) is built up, a new minister, *de novo*, has arrived. Thus the church of Christ extends to the east and to the west; and whether, by these means, the door of heaven will be opened for the Indians, who are blind of faith, and wild of manners, time will show. It seems as if God himself, looking upon this time of ignorance in these parts, proclaims everywhere for men to repent."

Hitherto, the career of Selyns, had been undis-

turbed by any opposing influence. Peace and pleas-
antness had uninterruptedly prevailed in his church.
The congregation had been fortunate in having an
able, zealous and godly minister, the minister, not less
so in an affectionate and confiding people. The cause
of the one had been the cause of the other, and both
had borne a common fate, whether in prosperity or
adversity. But the apple of political discord was now
to be thrown into their midst, and the harmony which
had affectionately existed until now was to be broken
by internal dissension, not to be thoroughly healed
during the remainder of his life. The wave of the
English revolution which placed William and Mary on
the throne, reached New York in May, 1689. The
city then contained a somewhat mixed population, as
to nationality. The Dutch still maintained their
ascendency in numbers, retaining the feelings of their
ancestors against the power of the papal see. Next
to them were the French Huguenots, who both before
and after the revocation of the edict of Nantz, had
taken up their abode in the city and adjacent villages,
to escape the persecution of Louis XIV. Many of
them, especially the earlier emigrants to the colony,
had, like the pilgrims of New England, passed first
into Holland and sojourned there before embarking
for this country; while Holland herself had become
an object of hostility of the French king, in consequence of affording an asylum to these persecuted
protestants, and for that reason they left her shores for

New York. There was on the part of both the Dutch
and French inhabitants a sympathetic dread of catholic influence. The popular mind was thus already
prepared when the news of the revolution reached
here, for the outbreak, having for its object the deposi-
tion of the governor and council of James, and
which resulted in placing Jacob Leisler at the head of
the government. But while the popular feeling ran
strongly in favor of installing a new governor, the
Dutch clergy denied the necessity of such a course.
The principal men of wealth and influence in the
colony were opposed to it; and the ministers were
naturally in sympathy with them. Some of these
men occupied places under the old government.
Stephen Van Cortlandt and Nicholas Bayard, members of the kings council, and Peter Schuyler, mayor
of Albany, were members of the Protestant Dutch
church, and by birth of the same country as King
William himself. It was idle to suppose, as the Leislerians charged, that these persons or the Dutch
clergy were inclined to favor papal power, when by
birth and religion they must have been in favor of the
prince of Orange. There was, therefore, sufficient
ground in the first instance, at least, for the course of
the Dutch clergy. All men of reflection, conserva-
tive feelings and quiet habits like ministers of the
gospel, would naturally refuse their sanction to the
usurpation of authority under such circumstances.
Besides, there were strong personal objection to Leis-

ler. He was not their countryman. He was not a
Dutchman, but was a German from Frankfort, a mere
adventurer, who had by industry and prudence, after
leaving the military service of the West India Company, in which he had been engaged as a common
soldier, acquired considerable property, and the influence which wealth begets. He was an unlettered
man. The ministers had no bond of nationality or of
social sympathy with him. But it must be confessed,
that whatever reason Selyns and his colleagues had, at
the outset, in opposing his government, they committed
a great error in continuing their opposition after its
establishment. The popular heart was with Leisler.
He represented three-fourths or more of the whole
population, Dutch as well as English. He was in fact
governor from the first by the voice of the people ;
and when the king's government addressed their
despatch, which arrived in December, 1689, to the
colonial government here, " to such as *for the time being*
takes care for preserving the peace, and administering
the laws in his majesty's province of New York,"
thereby admitting the probable if not certain deposi-
tion of the former government, and acknowledging,
by royal act, the existing authority, whatever it might
be, he became governor of right. Opposition to his
government became worse than folly — it was treason ;
and Leisler was entirely justified in adopting the
vigorous measures which he resorted to in order
to put it down. The Dutch ministers preaching

hostility to his authority were proper objects of his attention, and he did not hesitate to bestow it upon them. Dellius, who had influenced the minds of the people of Albany against him, was summoned to New York; but he fled to Boston, and remained there until the storm blew over. Varick, minister of the churches on Long Island, who openly preached against the revolution, escaped to New Castle, on the Delaware; but soon returning was arrested at his house in Flatbush, by order of Leisler, dragged to prison, tried and convicted under an indictment for treason, and sentenced to be deposed from his ministerial functions. Selyns remained at his post, the only Dutch clergyman on duty in the province for a considerable time, as Tesschenmaker was massacred at Schenectady, in February, 1690, and Van der Bosch, of Kingston, had been deposed the year before. Selyns had committed no overt act, rendering himself amenable to the law, but he was in such close communication and sympathy with the leaders of the opposition, that he was constantly watched. He was suspected of concealing Bayard, and his house was searched by public officers for the purpose of discovering him. His service in church, of which Leisler was a member, was interrupted by Leisler himself, who there threatened openly to silence him. His letters to Holland and elsewhere were stopped in transit and opened by order of the government. His feelings of hostility to Leisler were aggravated, no doubt, in a large degree by these circumstances, and were carried by him to the grave itself. He was one of those who approved and recommended the carrying into execution the sentence of that popular leader, when Sloughter wisely hesitated, and desired to wait until he could obtain the views of the home government on the propriety of the act. While Leisler was lying in prison, the helpless subject of a political prosecution, and the proper object of consolation from the ministers of religion, Selyns preached a sermon against him, from the verse of the Psalmist; " I had fainted unless I had believed, to see the goodness of the Lord in the land of the living." This proceeding on his part was, in the mildest view of the case, most injudicious and unwise. His opposition had already estranged from him the Leislerian portion of his congregation. He affected to call them men of inconsiderable influence. They, nevertheless, refused to contribute to his salary; and the refusal continued under this fresh provocation for several years. He appealed to the classis to interfere, and even sought through that body the mandate of King William, supposing, that, as a Dutchman, he could be induced by the ecclesiastical authorities at Amsterdam to compel the payment of his arrears. He intimated that he would in consequence of withholding the salary be forced to give up his ministry here and return to Holland. The classis, in a proper spirit, advised him to pacify and win back the alienated hearts of his flock, and to

suffer and forget all in love; and also addressed a
letter in the same spirit to the consistory and congregation. The difficulty was thus finally arranged.
The divisions which the acts of Leisler and his party
had created among the people continued, however,
for many years to embitter their minds against each
other. They were the foundation of the political
controversies which arose in the colony for more than
a generation afterwards. Governors shaped their
policy to sustain those who were in favor of the proceedings against Leisler, or who were opposed to them,
according to their own predilections; the same spirit
sometimes brought the assemblies and governors into
collision with each other. And by that kind of personal sympathy, of which history furnishes so many
examples, disputes in the churches and elsewhere
long afterwards received their tone and direction from
the political views of the parties in regard to the
Leislerian government.

The first intimation of these troubles by Dom.
Selyns is in à letter of the 14th of September, 1690.

"Your favor of the 22d August, 1689, addressed
to Dom. Varick and myself, have arrived at last, and
greatly comforted and inspirited us. We will be
more encouraged by the *sauvegarde* of our King William and Queen Mary, who has probably too much
to do in England to think of us here. The Lord
bless their annointed majesties, and make them more

and more foster fathers and nursing mothers of our church, and defenders of the faith.

"I wrote last year to the Rev. Classis and sent, by Schipper Silke, an Indian bible with the psalms, which the French captured, and so never came to hand. I bought it in Boston, in order to transmit through it a memorial that we have been for sixteen years one of your classical assembly; showing how God, in order to convert the Indians, speaks the Indian language. But it is in these days to be apprehended lest we, who are called christians, may not be converted into Indians. We have been compelled to depose Dom. Laur. Van der Bosch, called from Staten Island to the Esopus. Dom. Petrus Tesschenmaker, the minister at Schenectady, has met with misfortune. He and most of his congregation were surprised at night and massacred by the French and Indians in their interest. His head was cloven open and his body burnt to the shoulder blades. Dom. Dellius who, to his great praise, has converted and baptized some Indians, has come down here from New Albany, intending to return home, and give an explanation of all to the classis. Dom. Varick and I, who endure more than can be believed, have to be patient of necessity. The Lord incline the hearts of their majesties to send some one over at last to this government, in order to heal the breach and quiet all. Without this, we are resolved rather to forsake all, and either return home, or, with Elias, to hide ourselves in the wilderness and follow the service of Jesus Christ, *ultra Garamantas et Indos*. Remember us in the prayers of the Rev. Synods of South and North Holland, and in the letters to their royal majesties. Pray for us, brethren, and for the peace of Jerusalem. The Lord bless you in your persons and in your service; and by his spirit of patience and forbearance support us, who would have written more, were it not that *our letters are, in violation of the rights of all persons, broken open and examined, and kept back from their destination.*"

The revolution interrupted the communication between Holland and New York, so that two years elapsed before we find any further reference by Selyns to his persecutions. Although he had written home, no letter had in the meantime been received either by him or the classis. It was to him a period of despondency and gloom. When, however, the *espionage* of the mail was removed by the introduction of regular authority, he wrote more freely on Leisler's government. Dellius and Varick united in the letter:

"Although we have for two or three years past written, informing you of the sad condition of our church and country, we have been unfortunate in not being answered, or in not having received any letters in reply. It may have been in consequence of the war, or of the troubles, worse than war, with a foreign foe, that yours have been taken by the enemy, or ours

have been kept back here. Ministers have not been
permitted to write to ministers or to your reverences,
nor have private individuals been allowed to corre-
spond with their friends and acquaintances. During
this period, everything has been done ostensibly on
behalf of King William, and for the sake of religion;
but, in fact, contrary to law, King William and the
protestant faith. Our ministers have been calumni-
ously suspected; the people have been advised not
to contribute to the service or the support of religion;
clerks and schoolmasters have been encouraged to
perform the duties of the clergy; high councillors,
who were baptized elders, have been denounced by
the unheard names of traitors and papists; clergymen
and other members of our church have been apprehended, tried and sentenced to imprisonment, and
kept in chains and dark confinement. Nor was this
enough. The holy sanctuary has been attacked with
violence and open force. Dellius, no fool to allow
himself to be imprisoned, chose the hare's path and
fled to the south, to Boston. Varick followed his
example, and went south to New Castle. No one
remained to be troubled and plundered, except Selyns.
Varick returning home, was accused of *crimen læsæ
majestatis;* and Selyns offering himself and property
as bail for him, was refused, and threatened with
imprisonment himself. To write all that we have
unlawfully suffered would be tiresome, both to your
reverences and ourselves.

"There has come over here for governor Their Excellencies Sloughter, who is now dead, and Fletcher, the present governor, inclined to peace, and bringing with him the instructions of the king's council and the approval of the sentence, to the effect that Mr. Leisler and the rest were condemned according to law; and that their children having applied with all humility to their royal majesties, will be allowed to obtain and hold their property. Those in prison are to be set at liberty, upon submission and promise of good behavior. We who are without power, who are nothing more than servants of Jesus Christ, without any authority, are insulted, paid with calumny, and deprived of our own, receiving no salary worth specifying.

"In this year of troubles there has been built, outside of the fort, a new Dutch church, of stone, and larger than the old one, in order to bring to God and Christ Jesus many who had an antipathy to the fort. Varick and Dellius will be compelled to leave, and Selyns to live upon his own private means. Thus they endeavor to remove the candlestick, and to extinguish at New Albany the light for the conversion of the heathen. Bergen, Hackensack, Staten Island and Harlem, have fallen off, under the idea they can live without ministers or sacraments. Since Mr. Hobbe[1] has left Hempstead for New England, in

---

[1] Rev. Jeremiah Hobart is meant. The year of Mr. Hobart's leaving Hempstead is usually stated to be 1696.

His daughter Dorothy was the mother of David Brainard, the celebrated missionary among the Indians.

consequence of non-payment of his salary, and Dom. Van der Bosch, who was censured, has gone from Esopus to Maryland, we see no means by which those places can be supplied. We must not omit to mention that the two French churches have been united, and that Dom. Perrot will perform service in the city for the most part, and Dom. Daillè in the country,— all to be one church, and the income to be divided equally between them. Mr. Miller has come over as chaplain here, and Mr. Cox as chaplain in Maryland, persons of the requisite knowledge.

"Now we request your reverences to contribute all that is practicable for our good, and that of the church. Let our complaints, thus lying upon the table of your classical labors and commisseration, be taken up and gathered into the flask of the communion of the saints, and be transmitted to the Christian Synods. Should it not be made known either by your reverences or by the Synods of North Holland, or else letters written to the king in favor of the church and ministers? Should not the governor and council be written to, and informed that we were called with the knowledge of this government? Should not our elders and deacons, who have bound themselves by special notarial obligations, be reminded and admonished to make prompt and adequate payment? Should it not be shown to the same that the object is to have no more preaching, and to obtain the means of destroying both church and religion, to change Christians

into Indians, and to abandon the work of converting
the heathen at New Albany ?"[1]

With the administration of Fletcher commenced a
distinct era both in the civil and religious history of
the province. It is difficult at this day to decide
whether his commissions to the freebooters were the
result or cause of an influx of strangers into the city,
extending its limits but undermining its morals; yet
the one and the other fact are both true.[2] Tew,
Coates, and others, pirates pursuing their depreda-
tions upon commerce in the East Indies were shielded
by his written authority to privateer, while many of
the persons connected with them resided here. New
York became the centre of a large contraband trade
in consequence of the protection which his commissions afforded those engaged in carrying it on. Like
too many of the governors sent over to America
his avarice rendered him false both to king and
people. There were no grants within the power of
the crown to bestow which had not their price with
him, and he issued them without stint, when they
were sought for with adequate rewards. His enor-
mous grants of land, to private individuals, and his
charters to the Dutch church and Trinity church with

---

[1] Letter to the classis, 12th Oct., 1692.

[2] New York was at this time the resort of privateers of nations at
war in consequence of its convenience, where they obtained supplies
both of men and provisions. Stringent acts against enlisting in such
foreign service and for the arrest of pirates were passed by the
assembly, in 1693 and 1698.

great privileges, all, it was subsequently alleged, were
made through bribery and corruption, but of the
exact circumstances in regard to the Dutch church
we will have occasion presently to speak more particularly.

Fletcher's commission, giving him the power of
collation and suspension of the minister of any church
in the colony, was a power not within the prerogative
of the king in fact to confer, as it was one which the
sovereign himself could not directly exercise out of
England, Wales, Berwick on Tweed and the adjacent
islands. It was a power connected with the church
of England, which, as an established church, was the
creature of the statute which confined it to the places
just mentioned. That church was not the church of
the realm by common law, and no statute had ever
been passed by parliament extending it to America.[1]
Nevertheless, the power was attempted to be exercised,
as we have already seen, by the duke, and to be conferred now by the king upon the governors of New
York. One of Fletcher's first acts was to obtain from
the assembly a recognition of this power. He recommended to the assembly of 1692, that provision for a
ministry should be made by law. He renewed the
request in 1693, and an act was then passed for New
York, Richmond, Westchester and Queens counties,
providing for the settlement of ministers of the

---

[1] It was argued on the other side that as there was no statute
regulating churches in the plantations the whole subject rested in
the royal perogative of necessity.

protestant faith, to be called by officers to be elected by the people of the different parishes.   In its phraseology this statute looked to the establishment of the church of England, especially in the titles of vestrymen and church wardens, given to the officers who were to be elected for the purpose of choosing the ministers; but in truth there was no limitation upon the power of these officers which would prevent them from calling a dissenting minister, provided he was a protestant, as was abundantly established by the fact that Mr. Vesey, the first minister of Trinity church, was a dissenting clergyman preaching on Long Island, at the time of his being called to that church. Fletcher, however, quarrelled with the assembly and returned the bill because it did not give him the power of collation of ministers.

But the differences between the governor and assembly were the differences of the friends of the church of England and the English dissenters.   The Dutch churches were not in the arena of the strife. So far as the Dutch themselves were concerned they were between the upper and lower millstone.   Which ever party prevailed in the contest they were liable to pay their quota of church rates for the support of a minister, whether Episcopalian or Presbyterian, and whether they attended his services or not.   It was evidently not contemplated by the contending parties that a minister of the Dutch church would be called under the provisions of the act, for the counties of

Albany, Kings and Ulster, particularly, where the
Dutch population prevailed, were not subject to its
provisions. The city of New York, however, was
under its operation, though the Dutch church there continued to exercise its privileges without molestation.
Selyns was not satisfied with the legal condition of
the church. The pretensions of the crown in regard
to an established church showed that its privileges
might at any moment be withdrawn. It was in this
state of uncertainty that he and his consistory applied
to Fletcher for a charter, which was granted,— the
first church charter issued in the colony.[1] This
instrument secured to the church its independence.
It contained some extraordinary provisions. Besides
conferring upon the church the power of calling its
ministers, which was the really. great point to be
attained, and authorizing it to hold property acquired
by gift or devise, it provided for a compulsory payment of church rates for the support of the minister
and church by its members. These provisions were
considered by Selyns as fixing permanently the status
of the church ; and in fact this charter remained in
force up to the time of the independence of this
country of the crown of England, when by an act of
the legislature of this state it was confirmed, with the
exception of that portion of it relating to forced rates,

---

[1] This charter bearing date 11th May, 1696, may be found in the
office of the Secretary of State in book of patents 7, p. 25 It preceded that of Trinity church, which was granted on the 6th of May,
1697.

which it appears had never been enforced, but which was repealed as inconsistent with the principles of republican government.[1]   Governor Fletcher's successor, Lord Bellamont, sought at the time to have the charter vacated on account of its having been obtained through bribery, but without success, although it was not denied that the consistory had voted Fletcher a piece of plate as a present.   The charter of Trinity was superseded by act of assembly in 1704, but the Dutch church charter remained untouched.

The great object for which Selyns had long labored was now accomplished and he did not fail to announce the event to the classis, with some other interesting facts. He wrote on 30th September, 1696:

" We are supplied with ministers in all the churches and now number five Low Dutch ministers, namely, myself at New York, Dom. Dellius at New Albany, Dom. Nicella at Esopus, Dom. Lupardus on Long Island and Dom. Barthold in New Jersey.   The Lord grant that the service and administration be further extended in this remote land. My consistory and myself have in the meanwhile long labored and much means employed to obtain some privileges for the Low Dutch church here at New York.   This has now been accomplished very satisfactorily and fortified under the royal seal.   The title reads, *The Charter of the Reformed Protestant Dutch Church in the city of New*

---

[1] Act of 17th March, 1784.

York, granted Anno Dom. 1696. It authorizes the calling of ministers, choosing elders and deacons, chaunter and sexton, and establishing a Dutch school, all conformably to the Synodal canons of Dordrecht; also to own a church, a parsonage and all the goods of the church, as private property, to be held *corporaliter*, without power of alienation; also to receive bequests whether of fast or moveable property, or any thing by donation for the church or its service, &c., &c.,—a measure which will produce much good to God's church and put many things to rest.

"As to my arrears of salary, they are now all paid, and where we, alas! have passed sorrowful days, all things are put in better condition.

"There are many English ministers in the rural districts, mostly from New England and educated there, where much good is done. The university at Cambridge has graduated the past year ten more in philosophy and eight in higher studies. For the two English churches in this city which have been formed since our new church was built,—one of our churches being in the fort and the other in the city, and both of them very neat, curious and all of stone,—there are two Episcopal clergymen who by arrangement preach in our church after my morning and afternoon service, and live with us in all friendship. Dom. Daillè, late French minister here, has been called to Boston and ministers in the French church there. Dom. Perrot, a man of great learning, formerly a minister in France, serves God's church here, and Dom. Morse[1] in the outer villages. Dom. Brodet, late professor at Salmurs, having since lived and preached eight years among the Indians in their language, is called to New Rochelle, five hours ride from this place, and causes great edification by his gifts and life. Thus it is that God's church floats on the billows of a new world, which had much need of the prayers of the old. This country is not without losses caused by the war. Many ships belonging here at home were captured at sea in the West Indies. Morals have much degenerated and evil practices have been introduced by strangers and multitudes of privateersmen. And what is to be apprehended is that we may be surprised both on the sea and on land; as the French, our enemy, have attempted this summer to do from Montreal and Quebec in Canada. Our calamities spring from a bottomless pool of heaven-high sins; foreign but, nevertheless, without suspicion of foreigners. They lay out the city, build high houses, and make land into the water. Indeed, since I arrived here the last time the city and its inhabitants have increased more than two-third parts. O God, though like unto Sodom in our sins, let us not be like unto Sodom in our punishment with the rising sun."

With the consummation of the liberties of his church

---

[1] The Rev. John Morse of Newtown, L. I. is probably here meant. He was a dissenting minister.

Selyns had accomplished that period in his life when he was fairly entitled to be emerited, or at least to be assisted in his labors. He had now attained his sixtieth year. He had labored faithfully, zealously and successfully. Amidst all his trials no one had ventured to breathe a syllable against the purity of his life and conversation, or of his fidelity to the spiritual interests of his congregation, which had increased from four hundred and fifty to six hundred and fifty members during his ministry among them. The consistory, accordingly, after much deliberation, though it must be added with great opposition, finally, on the 21st of July, 1698, authorized the classis of Amsterdam to call in their name, as assistant minister, the Rev. Hieronimus Verdieren, of Bruynesse on the island of Oost Duiveland, in the classis of Zierickzee, to be in all respects clothed with the same authority as Dom. Selyns.

But the animosities engendered in the church by the Leislerian troubles were smouldered only, not extinguished. They burst out anew upon this act of the consistory, based upon the charter rather than upon the vote of the congregation. The charter gave the power of calling ministers to the minister and consistory; the practice in the church had been for the congregation to exercise it. A party, which it is easy to see were Leislerians, opposed this call. They wished to have a minister of their own party. The controversy was carried to the classis at Amsterdam;

but Mr. Verdieren wisely declined, under the circumstances, to accept the call; and in the exercise of the further authority conferred upon the classis in case of his declination, that body called the Rev. Gualterus du Bois, son of the late minister at Amsterdam, who arrived here in 1699, and immediately entered upon the duties of the place.

Dom. Selyns did not long survive this event. As had been anticipated by his consistory and expressed in their call for a second minister, he was approaching the end of his earthly career. He died at New York, in July, 1701, in the sixty-fifth year of his age, universally esteemed for his talents and virtues.

In his domestic relations he appears to have been fortunate. Of his first wife we have already spoken. Upon her death in 1686 he married the widow of Cornelius Steenwyck, Margaretta de Riemer, whom he himself describes as "rich in temporal goods, but richer in spiritual." This lady survived him several years. He had one child, a daughter, by his first wife, born while he was at Breukelen, but from all omission of her name in his will we infer she died while he was in Holland.

Although Dom. Selyns was in correspondence with many men of genius and learning he never appeared before the world as an author; nor has he left behind him any literary work, except the little volume of poems which has induced this sketch of his life, and the few occasional pieces published in the manner already mentioned. As he did not choose to lay before the world the poetical effusions of his pen, it would be unfair to apply to them the canons of severe criticism. They are presented now only as interesting from the circumstances under which they were produced. The reader will, however, find in the few specimens which we have reproduced, proofs of culture and genius, and in his epigrams a spirit of true humor.

His character, as we are able to view it through the long vista of time and with an imperfect exhibition of its traits, presents him in a favorable light. He was a faithful and devoted minister, honest, sincere and capable. He was learned in his profession, pious and pure in his life. He was free from that narrow feeling which begets prejudice from mere difference of opinion. But he was fond of the exercise of power. He was persevering, and pursued his object with determination, and sought it sometimes for the sake of success when perhaps a wise regard for the feelings of others would have led him to abandon it. He may be justly regarded as one of the founders of the Dutch church in America, who did more to determine its position in the country than any other man; and in this circumscribed field, in which the great business of his life was concerned, his fame must mainly rest.

POEMS.

GEDICHTEN VAN SELYNS.

BRUYDTLOFS-LIEDT

Voor Ægidius Luyck en Judith Van Isendoorn, Getrouwt den tweede Kersdag.

Stemme — *O Kersnacht.*

1.   O Kersnacht, lichter dan de dagen,
   Want Hij, die geen begin der dagen,
     Noch eynde heeft tot mensche wort.
   Godt was Hij, maer geen mensch te voren,
   En wort tot Bethlehem geboren,
     Als 't kruydt van guure koud' verdort.

2.   Dit rijchste kindt komt arm ter werelt
   Meer binnen, als na 't oog bepeerelt
     Met croon en koninglijcke macht,
   En maeckt geen wercks van grooten steden
   Slechts met dit slechte vleck te vreden,
     Daer 't licht schynt midden in der nacht.

3.   Een maegt blijft maeght, en wordt tot moeder
   Des saligmaeckende Behoeder,
     Die ons so crachtelijck behoedt,
     Dat wy geen doot noch duyvel schroomen;

POEMS OF SELYNS.

NUPTIAL SONG

FOR ÆGIDIUS LUYCK AND JUDITH VAN ISENDOORN, MARRIED
THE SECOND DAY OF CHRISTMAS.

AIR — *O Christmas Night.*

1. O Christmas night! day's light transcending;—
   Who no beginning had or ending
     Until He man became, was God.
   Then He who ne'er before was human
   Was born in Bethlehem of woman,
     When nips the frost the verdant sod.

2. This richest babe comes poor in being,
   More pearled within than to the seeing
     With diadem and royal power;
   He takes no heed of greater places,
   But that small spot alone embraces,
     Where light illumes the midnight hour.

3. A maid remaining is the mother
   Of our salvation-working author,
     Who so defends us by his grace,
   We either death or devil fear not,

4. Begeert men dese Vorst te zoeken;
Syn luyers zyn versleten doecken;

  Want Godt heeft 't vleesche aengenoomen
    En worstelt met dit helsch gebroedt.
    Een crib syn wieg, en hoy syn bedt.
  Syn throon is meerder, als de meeste,
  En wordt een mensche by de beesten,
    Wat is 't Hem tot een harde wet?

5. Terwyl men brengt dit kindt te voren,
Komt Luyck en trouwt met Isendooren
    Voor dese Chrystelijcke crib;
  En vindt, als 't jawoordt was verscheenen
  Vleesch van syn vleesch, been van syn beenen,
    Want Judith wort syn tweede rib.

6. Nu zoeckt hij Godt met kuysche minne.
Sy, die voor sulcke crib beginnen,
    Zyn beter als dit Bethlehem,
  't Welck Christo weygert plaats te geeven,
  Meer dat sy leven naer dit leeven
    Met 't kindt in 't Nieuw Jerusalem.

For God in Him became incarnate,
  And wrestles with that hellish race.

4. This Prince,— do they desire to find him?
They're worn-out swaddling clothes that bind him.
  A manger, spread with hay, 's his bed.
His throne is higher than the highest,
Yet he among the cattle lieth.
  What Him, to such a lot, has led?

5. And as they bring this child before them,
Luyck comes and marries Isendooren,
  Standing before this Christlike crib;
And finds when her consent is shewn,
Flesh of his flesh, bone of his bone,
  For Judith is his second rib.

6. Now seeks he God with chaste affection.
Who take before such crib direction,
  Are better than this Bethlehem,
Which Christ no resting place will give;
For they, the after-life, shall live
  With Him in New Jerusalem.

BRUYDLOFT TOORTS

Voor D. Ægidius Luÿck, Rector der Latynsche Schole tot Nieuw Amsterdam, en Judith Van Isendoorn, Opgestoocken kort na d' Esopische moordt, gepleegt te Wiltwyck door de Wilden, in Nieuw Nederlandt, Ao, 1663.

Hoe ras wordt 't minnevyer door 't oorlogsvyer
  geblust,
Want Mars comt qualyck om d' onnoselheyt te tergen;
  Oft 't lust Cupido niet, die vreede en liefde lust,
En denckt sig selven voor de wapens te verbergen.
  Hy merckt dan 't onvermacht en voorbedacht ver-
    raet,
En seyde; is dit recht so steelgewys te komen?
  Men heeft een vyandts hert en vriendelyck gelaet,
Maer 't past voor Absaloms en Joabs list te
    schroomen.
  Syn woordt en is niet koudt, en vindt hy op syn
    woordt,
Helaes! niet huys op huys van wildt gedrocht beladen?
  Niet kindt op kindt geroost? niet man op man ver-
    moordt?
Niet schuur op schuur verbrandt en swang're vrouw
    gebraden?
  Men wyckt dan, daer men wyckt, uyt Wiltwyck zy
    myn wyck,
En neemen, spreeckt dit wicht, myn cours na bosch en
    bergen.
  Voorts soeckt hy pyl en boog, maer waren te
    gelyck,

BRIDAL TORCH

For Rev. Ægidius Luyck, Rector of the Latin School at New Amsterdam, and Judith Van Isendoorn, Lighted shortly after the Esopus murder committed at Wiltwyck, in New Netherland, by the Indians, in the year 1663.

How soon the flame of war the flame of love
    destroys!
For Mars comes wickedly, the innocent to injure;
    Nor does it Cupid please, who peace and love enjoys,
And starts, at sight of arms, to hide himself from
    danger.
    He sees the treachery, unlooked for, but designed,
And says: "Can this be right, so stealthily to come in?
    They show a friendly smile, but cloak a hostile mind;
'Tis well to fear for Absalom's and Joab's cunning."
    His words are yet still warm, and does he not behold,
Alas! house after house, with Indian monsters posted?
    Child upon child burnt up? and man on man lain
    cold?
Barn upon barn consumed? and pregnant women
    roasted?
    They flee, each where he can. "From Wiltwyck is
    my home,
I go," so speaks the wight, "in woods and hills t'
    abide in."
    He bow and arrow seeks; but they had both
    become

Allengskens gaet de lust en coopmanschap te niet,
En daegelycksche quaet baert daegelycken quaelen,
  Hoe, sprack hy, was dit windt? 't zyn boode van 't
    verdriet,
Tot buyt der Wilden, die se hier en daer verbergen.
  Die sig tot paeren quyt, is syn gereedschap quyt;
Maer so hy niet by tyt gepast hadt op syn vlercken,
  Sy hadden hem gedoot, gequest op weggeleyt
Om voor de wilden oft aen de wilden fort te wercken.
  Nu sat hy dickwils op 't gebergte van Kats-kil,
En clagde, wie gy zyt, en vloecht geen huysche
    minnen,
  Tot Hymen strecht myn lust, en Echte staat myn
    wil.
Maer vloecht, wiens sinnen zyn, vervloechte en wulp-
    sche sinnen.
  Oncuisheyt, dronckenschap en snode hovaerdy
Zyn oorsaeck van dit werck, drye schryende landt-
    sonden,
  En jagen heyl en vrêe uw landt en rêe verby,
Door ongebondentheyt, wordt sulcke straf ontbonden
  Die long gewaerschout is, wort selden seer beclaegt.
Hy seyt dan; siet te rug en siet de aerde beeven;
  Hoe 't vyer daelt uyt de lucht, en 't landt van 't poch-
    iens waegt;
Oft vraeght, die leeven, wie berooft zyn van het
    leeven

The Indian's ready spoil, who here and there were
  hiding.
When he is robb'd of these, his weapons are all gone.
And had he not betimes unto his wings betaken,
  They sure had killed or wounded him, or captive
  borne
For Indian chiefs to serve, or Indian forts to work in.
  But quickly sat he on the mountains of Katskil,
And thus his woe bewailed: "Domestic joys ne'er
  bless you,
  Till Hymen tends my loves, and wedlock serves my
  will.
And cursed be you whose thoughts, whence wanton-
  ness doth issue;
  Uncleanness, drunkenness and base and sordid
  pride,—
The land's three crying sins,— this ruin have effected,
  And driven happiness and peace your land aside.
For gross debauchery, such punishment 's inflicted;
  Whose warnings often giv'n did little heed com-
  mand.
"Remember," he continued, "the earth how it was
  shaken,
  How fires fell from the sky, and small-pox scourged
  the land;
And then seek for those lives, whose lives have now
  been taken.
  Insensibly all trade and pleasure go to naught,
And daily wickedness produces daily evil.
  What wind was that?" he asked; "it is with
  sorrow fraught,

En spooren tot berouw, oft 't laest moet 't al betaelen.

Met dit en dat beclag verflyt het wicht syn tydt;

Dan vloog hy wederom, en vloog na stadt en dorpen;

Maer waer hy vloog, hy is syn boog en pylen quyt,

En hadt syn ambacht haest door moeylyckheyt
verworpen

Dit lucht hem by geval, hy vindt somwyls den pyl,

Gevallen op de weg, ontvallen van de wilden.

Hy neemt geen lang beraet, maer scherpste met
ter yl,

't Schynt, dat sy eenigsins syn lust en onlust stilden,

Maer laesten zyn te seer van d'eersten ongelyck,

Wie wordt door min verrucht? wie moet van min
versmachten?

En wat het zy, het set geen sooden aen de dyck.

Syn cracht is cleynder, en syn pyls van cleynder
crachten;

Oft dit is oorsaeck, datter weyniger getrout,

En meerder zyn verreyst heeft groot'lycks syn be-
dencken.

Ten zy dan, dat wien 't uyt den koop, die trots en
stout

Ten onrecht hoopte 't recht van eygendom te
krencken.

Gewelt omtrent gewelt, en dorst na Christen bloet,

(Daer dienstig was gedult) en past geen Christi schapen;

Of schoon 't onnosel wicht, noch winst, noch voordeel doet

't Is beter, dat men laet onguure kinders slapen,

Die wacht bequaemer tydt, spilt, wat hy spilt, geen
tydt,

En waerom al te laet, en niet by tydts te laeten.

And with repentant sighs; so 't all at last be paid will."
  With these and like complaints the rogue his time
     did spend,
And then flew back again, to town and hamlet hieing.
  But where he flew nor bow nor arrow had to bend;
And his vocation so with difficulty plying.
  It happened him by chance he soon his arrow found;
Dropped in the way it lies, just where the Indians
     lost it.
He hesitates not long, but has it sharply ground.
And this, it seems, his passion and displeasure soothed;
  Although the former is the latter quite unlike.
Who is by love enthralled? Who is he whom love
     stifles?
Whate'er love be, it puts no sods upon the dyke,
Its strength is feeble, and its arrows are mere trifles.
  If this the reason be, that fewer married are
And more do journeys make, is worthy of reflection,
  Unless it be, on their account, who boldly dare,
And wrongly too, the right of property to weaken;
  Who force on force employ and thirst for Christian
     blood,—
(When patience would have served), nor have Christ's
     flock in keeping.
  Although the harmless rogue nor service does, nor
     good,
'Tis best to leave the savage children sleeping.
  Whoever bides his time, he spends no time, what
     else he spends.
Why is it then too late, to wait the fitting hour?

Maer dat bevestight werd', na 's landts geleegent-
    heyt,
Het recht van hooger recht, en staet van hooger
    staten.

En treedt niet, van het wicht en rechte oogmerck af,
Ten laesten, schynt ons quaet en landtstraf te vermind-
    'ren;

Dan rysen nu en dan gevangen uyt het graf,
Dan sneuvelt 't wildt gedrocht, dan vluchten vrouw en
    kind'ren,
Dan wort 't majies verwoest, en wilden-fort verbrant,
Dan crygt men roers ten roof, dan brengt men seewant
    binnen,
Dan vliegt men door het bosch, en loopt men door
    het lant;
Maer sien geen vluchtelings, noch kans om eer te
    winnen.

Hoe dingt 't barbarescen volk door meenig tolck
    na peysen,
En tracht met cracht de rêe van vrede te beseylen.
Maer als 't Cupido hoort, hy comt en maecht syn
    eysen.
Of vraegt, wie heeft myn boog? en klaegt, waer zyn
    myn pylen?
Booswichten spreeckt dit wicht, wat boosheyt moet
    dit zyn,
Heb ick dan iets gedaen? moet gy 't dan my vergel-
    den?
Ten ware, dat myn boog ontstack verliefde pyn,
Ick schoot u na de maet, als gy Cupido stelden.

Sy geeven geen bescheyt, maer geven pyl en boog,
En soecken syn gemoedt met 't eygen goodt te stillen.

Since that is wisely fixed to suit the country's ends,
The law of higher law, the strength of higher power.
But Cupid's true design does not this point concern.
At last, our sufferings and punishment diminish;
The captives, now and then, as from the grave
return ;
The savage monster's slain; his wife and children
vanish;
His maize is all destroyed; his fort burnt to the
ground;
His guns for booty ta'en; his seewan fills our coffers.
They fly into the woods, wand'ring the land around;
The fugitives not found, no chance for glory offers.
Oft through interpreters, for terms the Indians sue ;
The port of peace to gain they earnestly endeavor.
When Cupid hears of this, he comes with great ado
And asks, " Who has my bow?" and wails, "Where is
my quiver?"
" What villainy is this, ye scoundrels, " cries the
wight,
"Have I committed aught, that you should thus
reward me?
Unless it be, my shafts do amorous pains excite ?
I shoot you only in the measure you regard me."
They gave his weapons back, but made him no
reply,
Seeking to hush his wrath by thus his arms restoring.

Hy neemt se metter haest, en licht syn boog om
    hoog,
En schoon iets sonderlings met 't wapentuyg te willen.
  In 't fort[1] staet ieder, en besest dit crygs-gebruyck,
Luyck siet te venster uit, en *Judith* staet beneden;
  Maer eermen 't siet oft denckt, hy schiet en trefte
    Luyck;
Noch syn verbondt-lust is met d'eerste schoot te
    vreden.
  Waer schiet hy, (vraeght het volck) waer was 'et,
    daer hy schiet?
Luyck spreecht niet, want hy voelt iets vreemt syn
    hert doorbooren.
  Terwyl men siet na *Luyck* en *Judith* opwaarts siet,
Hy schiet ten tweeden mael en trefte *Isendoren.*
  Dit maeckt dan veel gewoels, en baerde groot geluyt
Van galm en weêrgalm; want hy spreecken niet, sy
    schreeuwen
  Door 't gantsche landt; geluck den Bruydegom en
    Bruydt,
Geluck dat echte paer, geluck voor veele eeuwen,
  Geluck, en wat men roept, zy duysent mael geluck,
Na ziel en lichaam, en so hier, als na dit leeven.
  Van binnen zy geluck, en buytens huys geen druck,
En die ons geeft geluck, is machtig 't haer te geeven.
  Maer wy, die by dit wicht, verstaen noch kindt van
    Mars
Noch soon van Venus, noch d'onreynicheyt der men-
    schen.

---

[1] New Amsterdam.

He quickly seizes them, and draws his bow on high,
As if he wished to pierce some special mark above
    him.
  The fort, New Amsterdam, is now by all possessed;
While Judith stands beneath, Luyck looks from the
    embrasure,
  And ere they see or think, he shoots Luyck in the
    breast.
Nor does one shaft suffice his cov'nant-making
    pleasure.
  "Where did he shoot? where was 't he shot?"
    inquire the folks.
Luyck speaks not, for he feels something his heart is
    boring.
  As all look up at Luyck, so Judith upward looks.
He shoots a second time and pierces Isendooren.
  This great commotion makes and causes, far and
    wide,
Reëchoings of joy.   While speaks he not, the cry
  Resounds throughout the land: "Joy to the groom
    and bride,
Joy to the married pair, and joy eternally."
  "Blessings a thousand fold, attend them both,"
    they shout,
"In body and in soul, here and hereafter flowing.
  Joy fill the house within: no sorrow lurk without:
Who gives us happiness, the same on them bestowing."
  Now we, who from this rogue, do neither child of
    Mars,
Nor Venus understand, nor yet the ways of mortals,

Maer 't geen ons dryft ten echt, en maeckt van
    onecht dwars,
Ten besten van vermeent, en wast te samen, wenschen.

  Dat voor dit nieuwe paer zy vrede en salicheyt,
Dat *Luycks* ontloocken heyl, en Isendorens seden
    Ontluycken meer en meer en groeyen metter tydt,
En datse stervende besesylen' s Hemels reeden.

OP HET PREDICK-AMPT

Van Wilhelmus Nieuwenhuysen, door my ingeseegent tot
ten dienst J. C. in N. Nederlandt.

Hoe wordt Nieuw Nederlandt vernieuwt door Nieuw-
    enhuysen.
    Hy doodt den oudemensch, en spreeckt de nieuwe
      voor ;
    Houdt d'oude leer, en dryft geen nieuwichheden
      door,
En doet door nieuwe drift haar oude quaet verhuysen.
    En wordt Nieuw Nederlandt door Nieuwenhuy-
      sens trouw,
    En Nieuwenhuysen door Nieuw Nederlandts
      berouw,
Na 't Nieuw Jerusalem gevoert om nieuwichheden,
Wat kerck vindt meerden heyl, als door vernieude
    seden.

Save what to wedlock leads and from uncleanness
    bars,
Wish them the best increase, and joy within their
    portals.
May this new married pair, peace and salvation
    know:
The budding hopes of Luyck and worth of Isendooren,
    Develope more and more, and thus with time so
    grow,
They at the dying hour, the port of heaven may moor
    in.

ON THE MINISTRY

Of Domine Willem Niewenhuysen.

How is New Netherland renewed by Newenhuysen?
    He kills the old man off and then the new directs;
    He holds old doctrines fast and not the new
    rejects,
E'er by his new pledged zeal old error ostracising.
    Now is New Netherland by Newenhuysen's
    mission,
    And Newenhuysen by New Netherland's contri-
    tion,
Led to the New Jerusalem for new delights.
What church more safety finds than in renewed rites?

GEBOORTE-CRANS

Gevlochten ter eeren van Machtelt Specht.

SANG.

Siet de Stichtse Nimphjens loopen,
  Siet se swieren over straet,
Siet, se willen kroontijens koopen,
  Kroontjens, diemen gieren laet,
Kroontjens, om een maegt te geeven,
  Vruchtjens van een geestig breyn,
Daer de bloomtjens altydt leeven.
  Siet, hoe dat se vrolyck syn,
't Is een lust, te sien 't geweemel,
  Veel, die loopen in en uyt,
Veel, die singen, dat de Heemel
  Wêer klincht van het blyd geluyt.
And're lachen, wie mag 't wesen?
Dat se voor de koud niet vresen.

TEGEN-SANG.

't Is een, dit men moet besteecken,
  't Soetste diertje van de stadt,
Die geen quaet met quaet sal wreecken,
  Die voor 't quaet een schrick al hadt.
Toen se met haer pop noch speelde,
  't Is een beeldt van seedigheyt,
Die een afkeer heeft van weelde;
  Die een eerbaer leeven leyt;
Die seer haet het snood bedriegen;
  Die seer hoog de waerheyt acht;

BIRTH-DAY GARLAND

WOVEN IN HONOR OF MATILDA SPECHT.

STROPHE.

See the nymphs' of Utrecht flying,
  See them tripping o'er the street,
See them little chaplets buying,
  Chaplets for adorning meet.
Chaplets to a maid becoming,
  Fruitlets of a sprightly brain,
Where are flow'rs always blooming.
  See, how joyous is the train,
To behold them is a pleasure;
  Some are running in and out,
Many singing till the azure
  Echoes with the blithesome shout.
Others laughing; who's the being?
From the cold that they're not fleeing.

ANTI-STROPHE.

They are thus with garlands wreathing
  Th' sweetest creature of the town;
Who for evil no ill breathing,
  Evil sees with horror's frown;
Who, when with her babe she's playing,
  Image is of modesty;
Who, all wantonness bewraying,
  Leads a life of purity;
Who with scorn the base despises,
  Who the truth does highly prize,

Die niet om gewin sal liegen;
  Noch naer heylloos voordeel tracht;
Oft niet licht haer woordt sal breecken,
Is 'et, die men moet besteecken.

SANG.

Waerom doet men 't onder 't vriesen?
  Als de vruchtjens zyn verdort,
Als se reuck en smaeck verliesen:
  Als het landt verdorven wort;
Als ne hagel deckt de dackjens,
  Dackjens, daer men onder woont;
Als de sneeuw schent al de tackjens,
  Daer men mêe de meisjens croont,
Als een boom is sonder blaedtjens
  En het aerdtryck sonder cruydt,
Als men siet, dat uyt de saedtjens,
  Niet een aerdig cruydtje spruyt,
Waerom, daer se niet en leeven,
Moet men groene bloemtjens geeven?

TEGEN-SANG.

Vroeger is niet nut het gieren,
  't Is nu haer geboorte-dag,
Die men meest altyt moest vieren,
  Als het ys in 't water lag.
Wie sal eer na blydschap hoopen,
  Het is nu de rechte tydt,
Dat wy moeten 't ciergel koopen,
  Dat men zoecht na vrolyckheydt,

Who for gain no word disguises,
  Nor for mean advantage tries;
Her word lightly never breathing,
'Tis for her they're garlands wreathing.

STROPHE.

Why, when all are frozen under,
  And the fruits all withered lie,
Taste and smell ta'en thence asunder,
  When the earth appears to die;
When the roofs with snow are bending,
  Roofs, whereunder dwellings are;
When the boughs the sleet is rending,
  Whence with sprigs they deck the fair;
When the forest leaves are dying,
  And no herbage clothes the field;
When the seed, all dormant lying,
  Not a living plant will yield;
Why, when none of these are living,
Must they blooming flowers be giving?

ANTI-STROPHE.

Sooner not the decoration;
  It is now her natal day.
Ever comes the celebration,
  When the waters ice display.
Who shall sooner hope for pleasure?
  It is now the fitting time
For attire to spend our treasure,
  And in merriment to join.

Dat men laet syn droefheyt vaeren,
   Dat men 't geestig diertje giert:
Want 't syn heden twingtig jaeren,
   Dat 'et hier gebooren wiert,
Dat 'et quam, daer alle menschen
Waer een beter leeven wenschen.

TOESANG.

Is se jaerig, en niet eerder
   So laet vry uw vlechten staen.
Wenscht haer, 't gieren is niet meerder,
   Wenscht haer, dat 't 'er wel mag gaen.
Wenscht haer, dat se lang mag leeven,
   Dat se sonder kommer leeft;
Roopt; ô groote Godt wilt geeven
   Dat se hier uw seegen heeft.
Wenscht haer, als se komt te sterven,
   Als haer siel van 't lichaam scheydt,
Dat se mag een leven erven,
   Dat men houdt in eenwichheydt,
Dat se mag hier boven komen,
Daer wy voor de doot niet schromen.

                              Non quæ super terram.

All, of trouble, disencumber,
  This sprightly creature to adorn.
Twenty years she now doth number,
  Since the day she here was born;
Since she came where heaven's portal,
Is the aim of ev'ry mortal.

EPODE.

'Tis her birthday and no later.
  Let your garlands gaily fly;
Wish her ornaments no greater;
  Wish her all prosperity;
Wish her many days to live for,
  That she may no sorrow know;
Pray: "Upon her, Great Jehovah!
  Do THY blessings e'er bestow;"
Wish her, when th' immortal spirit
  Leaves her body here to die,
She may then that life inherit,
  Which shall live eternally.
That she may ascend to heaven,
Whence all fear of death is driven.

Non quæ super terram.

AEN MYN VRIENDT

Capt. Gerard Douw, zig onthoudende op syn lusthof buyten N. Yorck, toen hy genodigt zoude werden tot des
Heeren Avontml. en geen wagen was, om genodigt te kun-
nen werden.

Die eens voor al genoodigt zyt,
    O Douw! 't ontbracht ons aen geen tydt,
Noch wil, maer aen Apostels paarden.
    Te ver, om daer te voet te gaen.
    Eêr afteraeden, dan te râen.
Best, daermen spaert syn paerdt, dat ick myn
    voeten spaerde.

    Gekomen, reedt men elck, om best, .
    Nu rydt men niet, dan elck, op 't lest.
Hoe daelt de son! maer, is dit wonder?
    Men graeft, slaeft, slooft, en zoeckt 'et syn,
    Al meest dit al, tot schade zyn.
De weerelt ryst, Godts kerck en Godtsdienst
    leyter onder.

    Maer, runt, o pen! niet al te ver,
    Heeft niemant wagen, paerdt oft kar.
Ick koom tot uw en allegader;
    Genoodight werdt gy tot dit feest
    Daer niemant is genoeg geweest,
Daer Christus is uw lot, en Godt is onse vader.

TO MY FRIEND,

CAPTAIN GERARD DOUW, RESIDING AT HIS COUNTRY SEAT NEAR
NEW YORK, WHEN HE SHOULD HAVE BEEN INVITED TO THE
LORD'S SUPPER, AND THERE WAS NO WAGON BY WHICH TO SEND
THE INVITATION.

You are invited, once for all,
O Douw! 'tis not that time does fail
Or will, save on Apostles horses.
Too far it is to go on foot,
And easier to dissuade than not;
When each one spares his horse, to spare our feet
they force us.

They rode, and each came for the best,
They ride not now, each in the least;
The sun goes down. Is't any wonder?
Each digs, toils, moils, pursues his own,
And, to his loss, seeks that alone.
The world goes up; God's church and worship
going under.

But run, O pen! not on too far;
No one has wagon, horse or car;
I come to you and all together.
You are invited to this feast,
Where no one is too oft a guest,
Where Christ your portion is, and God's our
heavenly Father.

Myn ziel! hout op, en schryft niet meer,
Ten Heemel opgetrocken, Heer!
Wie zoud' niet komen, om te komen?
Ick koom, oft kost ick hoger gaen,
'k Zoud Jesus zien, en hoger staen,
En wagens, elck van vyer om Jesum te
bekomen.

Komt Douw, en toont myn groot verdriet.
Wie ziel oft wagens heeft, oft niet,
Niet meer, oft langer te verzoeken.
Is Jesus oft syn lyden niet?
O Douw! verthoont myn groot verdriet,
Zo dit is nietmendal, Godt stelt 'et in zyn
boecken.

't Gelooft, dat schult en straff' verdooft
Is meer dan wet en straff 't gelooft
Brengt ons, en u van hier na boven.
Doet dit en meer godtsalicheyt.
Gelooft en boet stelt zalicheyt,
Om 't samen Godt alhier, en Godt hier na te loven,

VOOR EEN POORT.

Gelyck ons veenlandt is,
Dat morgen geen landt is;
So is men, vol verdriets,
Nu iets, en morgen niets.

Refrain, my soul, complain no more!
Drawn up, O Lord! to heaven's door,
Who would not come, so there to enter?
I come, and could I higher rise,
I'd Jesus see; and mount the skies,
In chariots of fire, the Savior to encounter.

Come, Douw! behold my grievous woe.
The soul which wagons has or no,
Naught more or longer need solicit.
Are Jesus or his suff'rings naught?
O, Douw! behold my aching heart.
Though it be e'er so small, God in his books
does place it.

But faith, which sin and death destroys,
Is stronger than both death and laws,
It raises us and you to heaven;
Devotion does all this and more;
Salvation springs from faith and prayer,
Here and hereafter both, God's love to us
vouchsafing.

FOR A GATE.

Like as our moorland is,
To-morrow nor land is,
So 't is with woe begone,
Now some, to-morrow none.

GRAAFSCHRIFT

Voor D. Johannes Megapolensis, Predicant tot Nieuw
Amsterdam.

Nieuw Nederlander schreyt,
En spaert geen tranen, want
Megapolensis leyt
(Zuyl van Nieuw Nederlandt)
Hier uyt syn volle leden.
Syn onvermoeyde werck
Was bidden dag en nacht,
En yv'ren in Godts kerck.
Nu rust hy, en belacht
Des weerelts ydelheden.

GRAAFSCHRIFT

Voor Jw. Anna Loockermans wede. van den Heer Olof
Stephensz van Cortlandt, overleden den 14 May, 1684.
In Domine quies.

Hier rust, die sonder rust was tsedert Cortlandts
doot,
En zocht geen rust, dan haest en nevens hem te
rusten.
Hy stierf. Sy leest en sterft Men rust in Abrams
schoot.
En leest, waer Jesus is, in ware rust en lusten.
Was Anna[1] in Godts dienst, badt[2] Hanna met Godts
geest.
Maer dese was alleen, dat beyde zyn geweest.

---

[1] Luke ii, 36.   [2] 2 Sam. i, 10–11.

EPITAPH

ON DOMINE JOHANNES MEGAPOLENSIS, MINISTER AT NEW
AMSTERDAM.

New Netherlander weep,
　Check not the gushing tear.
In perfect shape, doth sleep
　Megapolensis here,—
New Netherland's great treasure.
　His never-tiring work
Was day and night to pray,
　And zeal in th' church exert.
Now let him rest, where may
　He scorn all worldly pleasure.

EPITAPH

FOR MADAM ANNA LOOCKERMANS, WIDOW OF OLOF STEPHENSEN
VAN CORTLANDT, ESQ., DECEASED 14 MAY, 1684.

Here rests who after Cortlandt's death no rest
　possessed,
And sought no other rest than soon to rest beside him.
He died. She lived and died. Both now in Abram
　rest,
And there, where Jesus is, true rest and joys abide in.
God's will did Anna[1] serve; God's aid did Hannah[2]
　pray.
In this alone alike, that both have passed away.

---

[1] Luke ii, 36.　　　　　[2] 2 Sam. i, 10, 11.

OP 'T CONTERFEYTSEL

Van D. Nicolaus Renselaer, Propheet van Carel II.
Koninck van Englandt.

Is 't Renselaer, oft niet?

Die Nêerlandt onderrecht heeft

Van zeegen en verdriet,

En Carels-croon verseght heeft

Zeer lang voor zyn gebiedt.

GRAAFSCHRIFT

NEDERLANDT.

Voor Petrus Stuyvesant, gewesen Generael van Nieuw

Stuyft niet te seer in 't sandt, want daer leyt Stuyvesant,

Die eerst was 't opperhooft van gantsch Nieuw
Nederlandt,

En gaf met wil of geen het landt den vyandt over.

So naween en berouw treft iemants hert, syn hert

Stierf duysentmaal, en droog onlydelycke smert,

In 't eerste al te ryck, op 't laaste al te pover.

OP EEN MODDERMAN EEN SACK-JE GOUTS OPBAGGERENDE.

Indien d'er wond'ren zyn, so is dit een der wonderen,

Dat my 't geluck komt, niet van boven, maer van
onderen;

Want daer ick bagger, niet dan stinckend dreck
en slyck,

Daer maeckt gebaggert gout my en myn kind'ren
ryck.

ON THE PORTRAIT

OF DOMINE NICHOLAS RENSELAER, PROPHET OF CHARLES II,
KING OF ENGLAND.

Is 't Renselaer or no,
Who Netherland informed has,
Of blessings and of woe,
And Charles's crown forewarned has,
Long ere he came thereto?

EPITAPH

FOR PETER STUYVESANT, LATE GENERAL OF NEW NETHERLAND.

Stir not the *sand* too much, for there lies Stuyvesant,
Who erst commander was of all New Netherland.
Freely or no, unto the foe, the land did he give over.
If grief and sorrow any hearts do smite, his heart
Did die a thousand deaths and undergo a smart
Insuff'rable. At first, too rich; at last, too *pauvre*.

ON A MUDMAN DREDGING UP A BAG OF GOLD.

If wonders ever were, then this indeed is wonderful,
That my good luck not from above, but come from
under will.
For where I only dredge for stinking mud and mire,
I and my children wealth do dredg'd-up gold acquire.

OP BAETSOECKENDE EN ONRECHT-
MATIGE SCHOUTEN.

Oft 't rechte schouten zyn, om wetten te beschermen,
Die weesen zyn ten last, en weduwen tot schrick,
En slocken dorpen in, en speelen met de ermen,
En weet ick niet. Een schout moet 't elcken oogen-
blick
Sig voegen na Godts wet en keyserlycke rechten,
Om 't quaet door 't sweert met recht en niet met quaet
te slechten.

OP 'T BANCKEROT VAN EEN
DOCTOR.

Maeckt d'oorlog banck-rottiers, 't en is geen oorlogs-
wonder
Voor coopliêns; maer, halaes! wat bracht den doctor
onder?
Was 't oorlog met syn vrouw? oft krygt hy geen
patjenten?
Oft lydt hy veel verlies van jaerlycksche renten?
Maer d'en pleegt buytens huys te lappen door de billen,
En d' ander binnens huys met brassen 't goedt te
spillen.
Ziet, daer de man en vrouw, om prys het geldt ver-
teeren,
Zyn rotten in de kist en motten in de kleeren.

ON MERCENARY AND UNJUST BAILIFFS.

If they true baliffs be, who for the law maintaining,
  Do orphans overwhelm, and widows terrify,
And hamlets gobble up, the poor with sport disdaining,
  I know not; but, I trow, a schout should ever try
To have the law of God and sovereign rights possess
      him,
The wrong with power by right and not by wrong
      suppressing.

UPON THE BANKRUPTCY OF A PHYSICIAN.

That war should bankrupts make of merchants is no
      wonder:
But what, alas! was it that brought the doctor under?
Was 't warfare with his wife? or did he get no patients?
Or suffered he great loss from some who do not pay
      rents?
The one outside the house freely expends the treasure,
The other wastes, within, the goods beyond all measure.
Behold the man and wife, by squandering so flagrant,
Are rotten in the box and mothy in the raiment.

VAN QUADE VROUWEN MET DE DERDEDAEGSCHE KOORTS.

De derdendaegsche koorts is een der grootste plagen,
  Maer vrouwen, stuurs en boos, zyn d'aldergrootste
    quaet,
Want 't vasten en gebedt kan 't eerste quaedt verjagen,
  Maer wat het tweede raeckt, 'k en weet geen troost
    noch raet
      Dan 't quaet met groot gedult te lyden,
      En d'eerste aenstoot te vermyden.

AEN-EN AFRAEDINGE ON WEDU-WEES TE TROUWEN.

AENRADINGE.

Vriest iemant, dat hy trouwt geen brudyt, die rechte
    maegt is,
  Oft, 'k weet niet wat, gevraegt is,
Die kies'een weewdtje uyt, en laet de vrysters vaeren,
  Voor die onseecker paeren.

AFRAEDINGE.

Maer zyn geen weduwees voor dubbelt wee te houwen,
  Met *wee du wee* te trouwen?
Des wat het zy, oft niet, wie kan nyt 't water drincken
  Daer andere verdrincken.

OF SCOLDING WIVES AND THE THIRD DAY AGUE.

Among the greatest plagues, one is the third day ague;
But cross and scolding wives the greatest evils are;
With strong and pray'rful minds the first will cease to
plague you,
But for the last I know not what advice to dare;
Except with patience all to suffer,
And ne'er the first assault to proffer.

REASONS FOR AND AGAINST MARRYING WIDOWS.

PRO.

Fears any one his bride lest she a virgin be not,
Or what he would, I know not;
Let him a widow choose, and let the spinsters tarry,
Ere in such doubts he marry.

CON.

To wed a widow, is it not to marry trouble,
And *woe with woe* to double?
But be this so or not, who can take water down him
Another had to drown in?

OP MEYDEN EN KATTEN.

En grage kat en trage meydt,
Baert huys-krakeel en geen profyt;
Maer meyden graeg en katten traeg
Zyn buitentwyffel grooter plaeg,
Want snoept de kat eens nu of dan,
Geen stuck, of 't meysje snoept er van,
En maeckt tresoor en kelder leeg,
Dus hoe men 't raemt, 't en is geen deeg.

'T GRAFTSCHRIFT VOOR D'ADVOT.
CORNELIS ALMELOVEEN.

Houdt op, die gaet,
Uw tredt en rêen;
Want dese steen,
Daer gy op staet,
Deckt d'advocaet,
Almeloveen.

CHRONOSTICON.
SPONSI RESPECTU SPONSÆ.

VIVIt Vena MIhI e VenIs, neqVe Vena VenenI
est,
Vena DoLorIs erat; Vena saLVtIs erIt.

ON MAIDS AND CATS.

A nimble cat and lazy maid,
Breed household feuds and are no aid;
But lazy cats and nimble maids,
Beyond all doubt, are greater plagues.
Once, now and then, the cat may eat,
But snoops the maid in ev'ry plate,
And makes the purse and cellar low.
How e'er it hits, *there is no dough.*[1]

EPITAPH FOR THE ADVOCATE, CORNELIS ALMELOVEEN.

Stop, traveller,
Your thoughts contain.
This stone does screen,
Beneath you here,
The barrister,
Almeloveen.

CHRONOSTIC.

OF A BRIDEGROOM IN RESPECT OF HIS BRIDE.

No poisonous vein, but a Veen out of veins, lives for
     me,
A vein of sorrow it was, a vein of safety 't will be.

---

[1] It is not right.

IN CARMINA.

JOHANNIS WILSONI, SEN. PASTORIS NEO BASTONIENSIS, QUÆ
NEO BELGICO GUBERNATORI CECINIT.

Tu, Reverende senex, vates sanctissime, lingua
   Numinis, antistos logis honorq. gregis,
Accipe responsum, quod at hac tibi mittitur urbe,
   Dumq. meo vestrum carmine carmen eget.
Nec satis est cecinisse iterum Bastonia plaudit,
   Vicinumq. facis carmen, adire solum.
Scilicet Isaiden sequeris, sacrosque poetas,
   Quotquot erant, summa dexteritate sapis.
Quemq. celebramus patrem, meliore celebras
   Sumptu, laude, manu, carmine, corde, fide.
Ille petit pacem, sed tu pro pace pecaris,
   Dumq. pia gaudes pace, beatus eris.
Fratrumq. studet fœdus componere, sed nos
   Unius in Christo fœderis esse refero.
Ille Deo Belgisq. novis moderamine erodest,
   Teq. dei atque hominum causa salusq. movet.
Cuiq. Curaçovium curæ est, lateque gubernat,
   Nil dextrâ est proprius, nil pietate prius.
Ille hominum pestem, quos vexat spiritus, odit,
   Sed tibi tota cohors fœda cloaca mali est.
Quos et Evangelii pudet, et lex enthea sordet,
   Aut nil sunt vigiles, fœdera, sancta Trias.
Cumque docent, commune malum est. Ecclesia praestat,
   Nec sibi, sed Christo vivere quemque decet.
Te mage miramur de zelo et codice sacro,
   Quaeque tui norunt, omnibus illa patent.

Præsertimque novo faciunt idiomate numen,
  Tum credenda loqui, tum facienda loqui.
Jam facile est Indis cœlestem pandere portam
  Et Neogentili voce ciere fidem.
Sed nondum, fateor, sumus hac in parte beati,
  Aut pro barbarico semine nullus adest.
Ne tamen accusor culpæ, Wilsone, nec omnes
  Aut ausam, aut summam religionis habent.
Id vero pro parte tua est, Neo Anglia vicit,
  Et qui sunt victi, sedulitate docet.
Sique atras igitur furias Stuvesantius armis
  Frænet, forte spei janua major erit.
Hinc justi posco belli fideiq. triumphum,
  Meque tibi et Christo vivere juro. Vale.
  Scriptum Neo Amstela'd.

EPITAPHIUM MEUM.

Ætas si qua roget; cujum, Seline, sepulchrum est?
Dum sileo, præstat quemque silere, meum est.

NOTES.

I.

PAGE 133.

Ægidius Luyck and Judith Van Isendoorn.

Ægidius Luyck came to New Amsterdam in January, 1662, for the purpose of instructing the sons of Governor Stuyvesant. He was then twenty-one years of age, and, though young, bore the title of domine or reverend; but he was merely a theological student at that time. Indeed it does not appear that he ever officiated as a minister of the gospel. Immediately upon his arrival here he took charge of the Latin school which had been established in the colony three years before. Two years afterwards the city was surrendered to the English, and in 1665 he visited Holland in company with Governor Stuyvesant, who went there to vindicate his course in giving up New Amsterdam, and, by consequence, the whole colony of New Netherland, to the enemy, without resistance. Luyck returned to New Amsterdam before Stuyvesant and while it was under the English rule, and sympathizing strongly with the Dutch interest was appointed by Governor Colve, upon the retaking of the city in 1673 by the Dutch under Benkes, one of the commissioners to appraise the estates of the inhabitants. He was in fact a burgomaster at the time of the recapture and as such signed the articles of capitulation, no doubt very gladly, on the part of the city. When, on the final restoration of the colony to the English, the inhabitants were required to take the oath of allegiance to the new government, Luyck refused to do so, and soon after left the country, finally, for the fatherland.

Of the bride still less is known. It appears, however, from the records of the Dutch church in New York, that she came from

Deventer in Guelderland.   There is reason to believe that she was a
member of the family of Governor Stuyvesant, not only from the
fact stated in the lines of Domine Selyns that she resided in the fort,
where probably the governor at that time lived, but from the way in
which a person of the same name,— certainly not her, but probably
her mother or aunt,— is mixed up with the Stuyvesant family in the
early records.   In a list furnished by Dr. De Witt, and to be found in
2d series of *New York Hist. Coll.*, I, 398, of church members made in
1680 by Domine Selyns, is the following entry: "Juffrouw Judith
Isendoorn, widow of Peter Stuyvesant."   We have seen the original
and find this is a correct copy of the minute of Domine Selyns.
It presents a problem difficult to solve.   The name of the wife
and widow of Governor Stuyvesant was Judith Bayard.   It is
barely possible that she came from Isendoorn, which is a small
village in Guelderland, near Tiel, and hence may have borne the name
of Isendoorn.   She survived the governor, and her will is to be
found of record in the office of the surrogate of New York.   Mr.
Valentine complicates the difficulty in his manual of the corporation
of New York for 1862, by stating that it appears from her will that
her name was Isendoorn.   He is certainly wrong.   We have care-
fully examined the will and cannot discover in it the least authority
for that statement.

But there is abundant evidence that there was a Judith Isendoorn
or Van Isendoorn who was a different person from Judith Bayard the
wife of Governor Stuyvesant.   It is in the record of baptisms still
preserved by the Dutch Reformed Collegiate church of the city of
New York.   There were three children of the marriage of Ægidius Luyck and Judith Van Isendoorn born in New Amsterdam.
At the baptism of the first one, Catharyntie, on the 2d of
November, 1664, Petrus Stuyvesant and Judith Bayard are
named as witnesses.   At the baptism of Gideon, the second
born, on the first of September, 1671, Judith Isendoorn and
Judith Stuyvesant are named as witnesses; and at the baptism
of the third child, Cornelius Jacob, on the 13th of August, 1673,
Jacobus Backer and Judith Isendoorn were present as witnesses.

These entries indicate pretty clearly that Judith Isendoorn and Madame Stuyvesant were different parties, as well as the fact that there was probably some family connection between them. It might be supposed that the Judith Isendoorn here named was the spouse of Luyck and the mother of the children; but we find in an entry of the baptism of Catharine, the daughter of Nicholas William Stuyvesant (son of the governor) and Maritje Beekman, in 1678, when Madame Luyck had left the country and gone back to Holland with her husband, that at this baptism Judith Van Isendoorn was a witness; thus showing that there was another person of the name residing in New Amsterdam, neither the wife of Ægidius Luyck nor the widow of Governor Stuyvesant.

II.

Page 137.

The Massacre of the Dutch by the Indians at Esopus.

The massacre by the Indians of the Dutch settlers at Wiltwyck, now Kingston, Ulster county, so circumstantially narrated in this poem, took place on the 7th of June, 1663. The horrors of the transaction are not exaggerated here. Twenty-one persons were killed and fifty-five led away captive, besides some being wounded. It took place at noonday, while the men mostly were in the fields, who were shot down as they rushed homeward to their burning dwellings, which the savages had set fire to, after entering them carelessly under the pretence of selling maize and beans to the women. The minister of the place, Rev. Mr. Blom, wrote to the classis of Amsterdam a letter which in brief describes the awful barbarity of the Indians. " The burnt bodies," he says, " were most frightful to behold. A woman lay roasted with her child at her side, as if she were just delivered, of which I was a living witness. Other women lay burnt also in their houses, and one corpse with her fruit still in her womb was most cruelly butchered with her husband and another child in their dwelling. The houses were converted into heaps of ruins, so that I might say with Micah, ' we are made desolate.'—" *O'Callaghan's Hist. of New Netherland*, II, 475, where a list of the names of the sufferers and an interesting narrative of the expedition of the Dutch against the savages and their punishment, together with the recovery of the Christian captives may be found. There are some interesting traditions in relation to this bloody affair, more fanciful, however, than true, to be found in Weiss's *Hist. of French Prot. Refugees*, Am. ed. II, 292.

III
Page 139.

" Remember," he continued, " the earth how it was shaken,
How fires fell from the sky and small-pox scourged the land."

Of the portents,— the earthquakes, meteors and sickness, mentioned by the poet as foretokening the massacre, no account of their nature or extent, or indeed of their occurrence in New Netherland, has come down to us, with the exception of mention that the small-pox raged with great mortality at the time indicated, both among the Dutch and Indians. Still, the statement of Domine Selyns as regards the earthquakes and meteoric phenomena, is amply corroborated by the French and English annalists of Canada and New England. They were felt and witnessed throughout the whole of Canada particularly, where they were the most terrific ever known, and produced the greatest changes in the face of the earth any where mentioned in history. Clavigero, who derived his information from reliable sources, as we will presently see, sums up these extraordinary results in his history of Mexico, in these words: " The earthquake which was felt in Canada in the year 1663 overwhelmed a chain of mountains of freestone more than three hundred miles long, the whole of that immense tract being changed into a plain."[1] He does not give his authority and his statement has, therefore, been considered by those who have not investigated the subject, as quite

[1] Cullen's Clavigero, II, 221.

apochryphal. But the testimony of Father Hierosme Lalemant, who was present in Canada at the time, and the existing vestiges of the convulsion, abundantly establish the facts. The account of the Jesuit missionary sent from Quebec, is very interesting. "The heavens began," he writes, " with beautiful phenomena; the earth followed with furious upheavings which gave us to understand that these spirits of the air, mute and brilliant, were not mere empty signs, since they presaged to us convulsions which were about to make us tremble, in causing the earth to tremble. We have seen, since the last autumn, flaming serpents which interlaced themselves with each other in the form of the caduceus and flew through the air on wings of fire. At Quebec we saw a large globe of flame which made the night quite as light as day, only the sparks which it sent forth in every direction mingled terror with the pleasure which we experienced in looking at it. The same meteor appeared at Montreal, but it seemed to come out of the bosom of the moon, with a noise equal to that of cannon or thunder, and after traversing three leagues in the air finally disappeared behind the large mountain which gives its name to this island. But what seemed most extraordinary to us was the apparition of the three suns. It was a fine day last winter, and about eight o'clock in the morning, that a light, almost imperceptible, vapor rose from our great river, and when struck by the rays of the sun became transparent, but in such a manner that it had sufficient body to sustain the two images which this planet depicted upon it. The three suns were almost in a strait line, distant several fathoms apart, the real sun being in the middle. All three were crowned by a rainbow, whose colors were not well defined, now appearing like those of the Iris, then of a luminous white as though there were below an excessively strong light. This sight lasted nearly two hours the first time it appeared, which was on the seventh of January, 1663; and the second time, which was on the fourteenth day of the same month, it did not last so long, but only until the colors of the Iris having become dissipated by degrees, the two suns on the sides vanished also, leaving the one in the middle, as it were victorius." He then speaks of an eclipse of the sun on the first day of September, 1663, "which rendered the forests pale, sombre and melancholy." It began at 24 min. 42 sec. past 1 P. M. and ended at 52 min. 44 sec. past 3. The Father describes the earthquake which followed with great particularity. It began on the fifth of February, 1663, at about half past five o'clock in the afternoon, and the rumbling it caused was heard *at the same time* throughout the whole of Canada. He brings the fearful scene vividly before the mind of the reader. "The walls of the houses sway to and fro, the stones all shaking as if they were loose; the roofs bend first on one side and then on the other: the bells ring of themselves; the beams, rafters and floors crack; the earth bounds, causing the stakes of the palisades to dance; every one rushes out; the cattle run wild; children cry in the streets; men and women affrighted know not where to take refuge; some, prostrated on their knees in the snow, implore mercy, others pass the rest of the night in prayer,— the earthquakes continuing all the time with a certain rolling like that of ships on the sea, and causing in some the same sickness at the stomach as is felt on the water. In the forests the disorder was still greater. It seemed as if there were a struggle between the trees which knocked against each other; the trunks were detached, leaping up and down in such confusion and fracas that our Indians declared the whole forest was drunk. There was war among the mountains, some thrown up and upon others, leaving deep abysses, and in some cases burying trees in the earth to their very tops, and in others turning the branches down so that there was left only a forest of upturned trunks. Ice several feet deep broke, flying into pieces, and opening fissures from which issued thick clouds of smoke or jets of mud and sand high in the air; springs ceased to run or gave forth water impregnated with sulphur; rivers either disappeared or became entirely corrupted, the waters of some becoming yellow and others red; while those of the St. Lawrence became whitish as far down as Tadoussac." The accounts from Montreal, the Three Rivers and other places gave the same descriptions. "According to several of our Frenchmen and Indians, eyewitnesses, far up on the river of Three Rivers, five or six leagues from here, the banks which border the river in several places, of a prodigious height, have become level, having been razed from their

foundations and uprooted to the level of the water; these two mountains with all their forests having been overturned into the river,
forming a dam which compelled the river to change its bed and
spread itself over large plains, and the earth which had been under-
mined tumbling into it and mingling with its waters, which are still
so thick and troubled with it that they change the color of the entire
river of the St. Lawrence. Imagine how much earth must be necessary in order to continue to fill this body of water for three months
always full of mud. Fields are seen of more than a thousand acres
entirely flat, and as though they had been probably ploughed in the
same place where there were before only forests. At Tadoussac a
shower of ashes was seen which traversed the river like a heavy
storm. In the direction of the bay of St. Paul there was a little
mountain situated on the border of the river, about a quarter of a
league in circumference, which sunk, and then, as if it had only dived,
came up again from the bottom of the water to change itself into a
little island; and lower down towards the Point of Larks (aux Aloü-
ettes) an entire forest having become detached from the main land
glided into the river, showing large trees upright and blooming
which have arisen in the water in one day. These earthquakes
lasted till in the month of August, that is, more than six months; in
the moutains which lay behind, the noise and trembling were per-
petual; in other places there was usually a trembling two or three
times a day. In extent we believe it to have been universal through
all New France, for we learn it was felt in the islands of Percée and
Gaspé, and also in New England, Acadia and other places; so that of
our own knowledge it was felt for a distance two hundred leagues in
length by one hundred in breadth — that is, twenty thousand superfi-
cial leagues of earth trembled at once, the same day and moment." [1]
In corroboration of this description of Father Lalemant we must
add here the evidences to which we have alluded, furnished by the
physical aspects of the country at the present day. They are
described in a paper prepared by Lieut. Baddely, who does not appear
ever to have seen the Jesuit relation, upon the geognosy of the Sa-

---

[1] *Relation de la Neuvelle France ès années* 1662 *et* 1663. Chap. I and II.

guenay country.   Having observed that in general both sides of the
Saguenay are characterized by a continuous chain of mountains
whose longitudinal outline is only slightly undulated while their pre-
cipitous sides are always towards the river, to which the chain is
usually parallel, that intelligent writer remarks: "It will not fail to
be observed that this slightly undulated outline which is characteristic
of both sides of the Saguenay, is at variance with the general direction of the mountain chains in this country and particularly with
those in its neighborhood.   The general course of the mountain
chains is northeast and southwest, that is, the same as the valley of
the St. Lawrence.   The valley of the Saguenay is from the north of
west and nearly at right angles to it.   It is therefore, a cross valley.
That the rocks on either side of this valley were once united there
appears very little reason to doubt; but water must have had very
little to do with separating them, at least in the first instance.   From
the slightly undulated character of the sectional outlines of this valley
it would seem to have once been filled by a continuous chain which
has been severed longitudinally by some violent catastrophe the nature
of which can only be surmised.   It is probable, however, that an
earthquake has affected this disjunction.   A great wave would not
have acted longitudinally, but transversely, or in the direction of
least resistance.   The insignificant streams which enter this noble
river have had little effect in forming it, and the operation of tides and
maritime currents, though more effectual, can only have been partial
and secondary."   *Trans. Lit. and Hist. Society of Quebec*, I, 79, 107–8.

The great earthquake is mentioned as being felt in New England
by Josselyn.   *Two Voyages to New England*, p. 271.

IV.

PAGE 147.

Dom. William Nieuwenhuysen.

This clergyman was a relative of Domine Selyns.   He came
over from Amsterdam in 1671, and from that time until his

death in 1681 was the minister of the Dutch church in the city
of New York. Dom. Nieuwenhuysen had a controversy with
Governor Andross in regard to the installation of the Rev. Nicholas
Renselaer as minister of the Dutch church at Albany, upon the
recommendation of the Duke of York, against the usages of
the church and the wishes of the congregation. Being summoned
before the governor and council he admitted that a minister
ordained in England by bishops, as Mr. Renselaer had been, was
qualified to officiate and administer the sacraments according to the
constitution of the Reformed Dutch church; but this admission was
manifestly no admission of the *right* of Renselaer so to officiate;
but it was in form only a concession, and satisfied the civil power.
It was probably this circumstance of his controversy in relation to an
Albany question, that has led Dr. Rogers in his interesting Discourse
on the Dutch church in that city into the error of saying that Dom.
Nieuwenhuysen officiated in 1675 in Albany as the colleague of Dom.
Schaats. The latter was, in the theological nomenclature of the parties
in the Dutch church at that day, a Voetian, while Dom. Nieuwenhuysen was a Cocceian; and an union of two such opposing elements
would hardly have been agreeable, to say the least, in the same
congregation.

V.

Page 159.

Domine Johannes Megapolensis.

The Rev. Johannes Megapolensis came from Holland to New Netherland in 1642, under an agreement with Kiliaen Van Rensselaer to
officiate as minister in his colony for six years. At the termination
of that engagement he took charge of the church at New Amsterdam,
and continued its minister until his death in 1669, at the age of sixty
seven.

The name *Megapolensis* is latinized from Mechlenburg, whence his father came into Holland and became a minister in the Dutch church, in charge of the congregation first at Egmond on the Sea and afterwards at Koedyk and Pancras in North Holland. Johannes being a proponant, was called to the Wieringerwaard in the classis of Alkmaar, North Holland, in 1634, and was its first minister; from thence to the joint congregations of Schorel and Bergen or Bergum, in the same classis, where he remained until his departure for New Netherland.

His son Samuel, who came over with him, was first sent to Harvard college, and afterwards to the university of Leyden, where he obtained his degree of Doctor Theologicus et Medicus. Returning to New Amsterdam he became associated with his father in the ministry of the church there, upon the recommendation of Selyns, and to take his place. He returned to Holland after the surrender, where he was called to the church in the Wieringewaard in 1670,—thence to the Scotch church at Flushing, in 1677, and finally to the Scotch church at Dordrecht, in 1685, where he continued until 1700, when he became *emeritus*. He was probably living in 1705, as Veeris, from whom we derive these dates, and who published his *Church Alphabet* in that year, does not mention his death. Domine Johannes Megapolensis, was a learned and pious man. While at Fort Orange he acquired the language of the Mohawks and preached to them in their native tongue. He wrote a *Short Sketch of the Mohawk Indians in New Netherland*, an English translation of which may be found in Hazard's *Historical Collections*, and in the *Collections of the New York Historical Society*, New Series, vol. iii, 143. The lines of our author sufficiently attest the esteem in which he was held as a minister of the gospel. Selyns had been associated with him on his first arrival in N. N. in 1662, and knew him well. He also published a catechism for the use of the churches in this country.

VI.

PAGE 161.

Domine Nicholas Renselaer.

Smith, the historian, alludes to the same prophecy of Rev. Mr. Renselaer, predicting the restoration of Charles II., and adds that the people of Albany had a high opinion of his prophetic spirit, and many strange tales about him still prevailed there in his time. Mr. Renselaer came over to New York in 1675 and sought a grant of the manor of Rensselaerswyck by reason of the transfer of the colony to the Duke of York. It does not appear clearly whether he was related to the family of the original patroon or not. He failed however in this object. He had been admitted to holy orders in England by the bishop of Sarum and officiated as chaplain to Van Goch, the Dutch minister in London. He was recommended by the Duke of York to Sir Edmund Andross for a living in the colony. He was accordingly collated to Albany, but he was looked upon with disfavor both by the members and clergy of the Dutch church there, and was soon involved in difficulties with both; though he did not live long to cause them trouble. He died in 1678. He married Alida, a daughter of Philip Pietersen Schuyler, the founder of the Schuyler family in this state. His widow became the wife of Robert Livingston.

VII.

PAGE 161.

Gov. Peter Stuyvesant.

The author plays upon the name of Stuyvesant. The original spelling of the name was Stuyfsant. The father of Gov. Stuyvesant was a clergyman, and in a list of members of the church at Berlicum, a small town in Friesland where he officiated, is this entry;

"July 19, 1622, on a Friday, am I Balthazar Stuyfsant with my wife and children come to live at Berlicum." The name is derived from *Stuiven*, to stir or raise a dust, and *sand*, being the same in both the Dutch and English.

We paid a visit to Berlicum in 1861. It is a small village in the northern part of Friesland containing less than two hundred houses, mostly small cottages of a single story in height, whose inhabitants live in a state of almost patriarchal simplicity and devote themselves to the raising of potatoes, apples and other fruit. But no trace of the Stuyvesant family was to be found there. The old church even in which the Rev. Balthazar preached had been removed, though a painting of it adorned the walls of the one which had taken its place. We obtained some particulars of the governor's father, however, while we were in Friesland. He came to Berlicum from Scherpenzeel in the southern part of the same province, where he was the minister previous to 1619. He left Berlicum for Delfzyl in Guelderland in 1634, where he died three years afterwards. He was twice married, first with Margaretta Hardenstein who died at Berlicum on the 2d of May, 1625, at the age of fifty. Governor Peter Stuyvesant was issue of this marriage, as also Annake, a daughter, and perhaps others. The second marriage was with Styntie Pieters of Harlem, on the 22d of July, 1627, and of this marriage there were born Margaretta (two of that name) Tryncke and Balthazar.

Dom. Selyns has made the burden of his epitaph for the governor, the surrender of New Amsterdam to the English, and apprises us that he died of a broken heart caused by that event.

VIII.

PAGE 167.

Chronostic.

Domine Hubert Beets married Josina a-Veen in 1659. The chronostic develops that year by taking all the letters of the couplet used to denote Roman numerals and adding their proper powers together. This is one of the pieces of the author, of which the translation in consequence of the word *vein* being the same in English, Latin and Dutch and being also the name of the bride, illustrates his practice of punning upon the names of the persons who are the subjects of his verses.

Seal of Selyns.

MEMOIR AND POEMS

OF

NICASIUS DE SILLÈ.

LOSSING —BARRITT

NICASIUS DE SILLÈ.

NICASIUS DE SILLÈ, or SILLA, who was first councillor in the administration of Governor Stuyvesant of the affairs of New Netherland, was a man of no ordinary attainments in literature and science. He was probably a descendant of the person of the same name who filled several important positions under the government of the United Provinces, as well as the municipality of Amsterdam, in the latter part of the sixteenth century. The identity of their names is, however, all the evidence in our possession to justify the opinion in favor of this relationship, unless indeed his title of *well born* renders the supposition more probable. The elder DE SILLÈ was a native of Malines, or Mechlin, in the Belgian provinces, which he abandoned on account of religious persecution at the time when Balthazar de Moucheron, Peter Plancius and other of his countrymen, for the same reason, fled to Holland, where they became doubly entitled to the rights and consideration of citizens of the Dutch Republic, by reason of the part they took in the struggles of their adopted country for independence of the imperial power of Spain.

The subject of this notice was a native of Arnhem, and came to New Netherland in the summer of 1653, bringing with him a commission from the West India Company as first counciller in the colonial government. In this commission he is declared to be an experienced and able statesman and soldier, and is instructed to reside at Fort Amsterdam, to deliberate with the governor on all questions of war, police or public force; to promote alliances of amity and commerce; to assist in the administration of justice, both civil and criminal; and to advise generally on all matters which might transpire in the colony. He appears to have enjoyed the confidence of the governor, whom he accompanied in the expedition to the Delaware against the Swedes. He succeeded Van Tienhoven in 1656 as fiscal, or attorney-general. He was also at the same time appointed schout or sheriff of the city of New Amsterdam. In this office it was his duty among other important labors to make nightly tours around the town. It marks the simplicity of the times to read his complaints, on one occasion, to the burgomasters and schepens of the city, of the dogs making dangerous attacks upon him while performing that service, of the hallooing of the Indians in the streets, and the boys playing *hoeckje*, that is, playing hide and seek around the hooks or corners of the streets, to the prejudice of quiet and good order.

He became one of the proprietors of New Utrecht on Long Island, where in 1657 he built the first house erected in that town. It was standing until within a few years past. It was inclosed with high palisades to protect it from attack by the Indians. He resided there in 1659 and in 1674, and probably until his death, of which event, however, when and where it took place, we find no mention.

He began the records of the town of New Utrecht, which are not only in his hand writing, but evince in different respects his literary acquirements. It is to these records that we are indebted for the few specimens of his verse, which enable us to present him as one of the poets of New Netherland.

De Sillè's closing days were clouded by domestic troubles, and he seems to have needed all the consolations of that religion which breathes throughout his poetry. He left three children, all by his first wife, a son, Lawrence, from whom have descended many bearing his name, now generally abbreviated into Sill; and two daughters, Gerdientje, who married Gerritse Van Couwenhoven of Brooklyn, and Anna who became the wife of Hendrick Kip of New Amsterdam.

GEDICHTEN.

HET AERDTRIJCK SPREECKT TOT SYNE OPQUECKERS.

Hoe lang been ick verracht door allerhande dieren
Van onbeschoste luÿd, van slanghen, en van mieren.
  Noit sach ick s'Hemels glans belommert door't
    ghebos,
   Soo dat uit mÿn niet goets, noch uit mÿ niet en wos.
Ick bleef wel moer van al, dat ÿder weinich achte
t'Verstickten oock in mÿn, wat ick te voren brachte.
  Maer heÿ een sonne-schÿn, een aenghename locht
  Mÿn nieuwen Adam gaff, ooch ander voedsel brocht;
Doen ick gheen naem en had, wist ghy m'een naem te
    geeven,
Van Utrecht omberoempt, een eere hooch verheven
  Om mÿne vruchtbaerheit; Nu wacht hier naermaels
    meer.
  Ick ben genoeg bepronckt tot mÿnes namens eer,
Door't koorn, en boom-gewas, door paerden, en door
    koeijn,
Door't vrucht, en mensch-geslacht, die uit mijn komen
    groijen.
  Dat noit te voren was, dat breng ick voor den dag
  Daer ijder uit profijt naer wensch uit treeken mag.

POEMS.

THE EARTH SPEAKS TO ITS CULTIVATORS.

How long, my worth, did creatures of all kinds
    eschew,—
The ant, the slimy snake, and th' uncouth savage crew.
  Shut out from heaven's light by the umbrageous
    wood,
  Did naught that I produced, e'er savor of the good.
Mother of all I was; but little did they care
If what I might bring forth did ever breathe the air.
  But heat and sunshine now—a bright and genial
    sky,
  Infuse in me new life and nourishment supply;
And when I had no name, you gave the name to me
Of Utrecht, unrenowned, for my fertility.
  An honor great this is; but bide my future fame;
  I now am satisfied by th' honor of my name,
By grain and orchard fruit, by horses and by kine,
By plants and by a race of men,—all growth of mine.
  What never was before, I bring to open view,
  So all may profit draw as they may choose to do.

Ick danck u die mijn hebt so eerlijck uit ghetoghen;
Bidt nu om zeging Godt met knijen krom ghebogen.
    Noit salt u schaadlijck sijn, soo 't kompt uit s' hartsen
      gront,
    Want Godt laet nimmermeer vergaen een suijvre
    mont.

NICASIUS DE SILLE,

cecinit.

GRAAFSCHRIFT.

Hier leidt de eerst geboort van Cortilliau verstoten;
De eerste van het dorp van Utrecht gesproten,
    Onnosel voort getult, onnosel wech gerucht,
    Godt geeft datmet t'geteel hier naa een beter lucht.

N. D. S. 1657.

GHESANG OP DE WYSE VAN DE 116 PSALM.

1. Godt stelt ons hier tot der Barbara spijt
    Tot sijnes naemens eer wilt vrolijk singen,
      En van perte met vreudt sijn lof voort bringen
   Soo sal hij wonen bij ons alle tijt.

2. Bidt dem dat hij ons sijnen zeging seindt,
    En ons door sijn genaede wil bewaren,
      Soo sal geen quaed gespoock ons wedervaren,
   Dan sullen wij in voorspoed krijgen 't eindt.

Thanks be from me to you who thus my worth
    display;
Upon your bended knees God's blessing humbly pray.
    You never harm shall know, if from the heart it
      spring;
For God will not let die, who faithful voices bring.

NICASIUS DE SILLE,

cecinit.

EPITAPH.

Here lies the first of Cortelyou from life withdrawn,—
The first child in the village of our Utrecht born;
    Brought forth in innocence, snatched hence without
      a stain,
God gave it being here, a better life to gain.

N. D. S. 1657.

SONG IN THE MANNER OF THE 116TH PSALM.

1. God sets us here until barbaric fell,
    The glory of his name, shall gladly sing,
      And from the earth His praises forth shall bring,
  So He with us may henceforth ever dwell.

2. Pray Him on us his blessings to bestow,
    Our lives preserving by His sovereign grace,
      So we no evil spirit e'er shall face,
  And may prosperity forever know.

3. Hij sal ons sterck maken door sijne kracht,
   Ons van noodtdruft versien, van vee vermeren,
   Barbaren en benijden aan ons weeren.
   Dareom valt hem te voet met alle macht.

4. De Heer verqueckt die sijn in druck en pijn;
   Want sijne bracht is groot niet uit te spraken;
   Dareom O Godt! wilt uwe hant uit steeken
   En staen ons bij die uwe kinders sijn.

5. Wij sondaers, Heer, vallen voor U ter peer,
   Versoeken U bijstant die wij vertrouwen;
   Onse hoeder sijt ghij in ons benouwen
   Dareom kompt U, O Heer, alleen de eer.

Nicasius de Sille

cecinit.

3. His power with strength shall always us endow,
　　Our wants to meet, our cattle to increase,
　　Ourselves from savages and foes release;
　For which to Him devoutly let us bow.

4. He comforts who in pain and sorrow are;
　　His pow'r is inexpressible and grand.
　　O God! stretch out to us Thy helping hand,
　And keep Thy children in Thy tender care.

5. Sinners, O Lord, we bow before Thy throne,
　　Implore Thy aid, in which our trust we place;
　　Thou our protection art in our distress;
　The glory, Lord, we give to Thee alone.

　　　　　　　　　　NICASIUS DE SILLE,
　　　　　　　　　　　　cecinit.

INDEX.

LIST OF SUBSCRIBERS.

————◄••••►————

1	JAMES LENOX;	New York.
2	ANDREW BROWN;	Middletown, N. J.
3	THEODORE S. PARKER;	Hoboken, N. J.
4	JOHN V. L. PRUYN;	Albany.
5	ERASTUS CORNING;	Albany.
6	CHARLES I. BUSHNELL;	New York.
7	NEW YORK STATE LIBRARY;	Albany.
8	JOEL MUNSELL;	Albany.
9	WILLIAM A. YOUNG;	Albany.
10	ROBERT H. WATERMAN;	Albany.
11	ALMON W. GRISWOLD;	New York.
12	FRANCIS B. HAYES;	Boston.
13	GEORGE FOLSOM;	New York.
14	S. ALOFSEN;	Jersey City, N. J.
15	SAMUEL L. M. BARLOW;	New York.
16	ABRAM E. CUTTER;	Charlestown, Mass.
17	FRANK H. LITTLE;	Albany.
18	WILLIAM F. FOWLE;	Boston.
19	ALFRED WILD;	Albany.
20	JOHN A. McALLISTER;	Philadelphia.
21	MELANCTHON M. HURD;	New York.
22	THOMAS H. MORRELL;	New York.
23	EDWARD DeWITT;	New York.
24	AUG. TOEDTEBERG;	New York.

25 WILLIAM GOWANS;   New York.

26 WILLIAM L. ANDREWS;   New York.

27 ROBERT LENOX KENNEDY;   New York.

28 GEORGE BRINLEY;   Hartford.

29 JOHN F. McCOY;   New York.

30 BENJAMIN R. WINTHROP;   New York.

31 CHARLES B. COTTEN;   New York.

32 PENNSYLVANIA HISTORICAL SOCIETY; Philadelphia.

33 HENRY B. DAWSON;   Morrisania, N. Y.

34 ELIAS DEXTER;   New York.

35 N. H. JORALEMON;   Hoboken, N. J.

36 JAMES T. GIBERT, M. D.;   New York.

37 FERDINAND J. DREER;   Philadelphia.

38 JAMES M. BRUCE;   New York.

39 SAMUEL G. DRAKE;   Boston.

40 T. A. BISHOP;   New York.

41 CHARLES H. HART;   Philadelphia.

42 SAMUEL S. PURPLE, M. D.;   New York.

43 HENRY T. DROWNE;   New York.

44 WILLIAM A. WHITEMAN;   Philadelphia.

45 JOHN FOWLER, JR.;   New York.

46 MERCANTILE LIBRARY ASSOCIATION; New York.

47 ELI FRENCH;   New York.

48 R. W. BLEECKER;   New York.

49 FRANCIS S. HOFFMAN;   New York.

50 RICHARD W. ROCHE;   New York.

51 GEORGE CLASBACK;   New York.

52 J. K. WIGGIN;   Boston.

53 H. R. STILES, M. D.;   Brooklyn, N. Y.

54 HENRY BRADSTREET;   New York.

55 JOHN M. KEESE;   Rhinebeck.

56	WILLIAM E. SEDGWICK;	Lenox, Mass.
57	J. H. HICKCOX;	Albany.
58	WILLIAM BROTHERHEAD;	Philadelphia.
59	ALEXANDER FARNUM;	Providence.
60	W. ELLIOT WOODWARD;	Roxbury, Mass.
61	JOHN M. BRADSTREET;	New York.
62	D. WILLIAMS PATTERSON;	W. Winsted, Conn.
63	C. B. RICHARDSON;	New York.
64	JOSEPH SABIN;	New York.
65	GEORGE W. WALES;	Boston.
66	J. P. PUTNAM;	Boston.
67	EDWARD DEXTER;	New York.
68	J. HAMMOND TRUMBULL;	Hartford, Conn.
69	G. A. SOMERBY;	Boston.
70	CHARLES E. WEST;	Brooklyn, N. Y.
71	GEORGE P. PHILES;	New York.
72	T. A. EMMET, M. D.;	New York.
73	JOHN W. MILLS;	White Plains, N. Y.
74	JOHN S. H. FOGG, M. D.;	Boston.
75	E. B. O'CALLAGHAN, M. D.;	Albany.